"THANK GOD FOR TEEN CHALLENGE!"

"I've believed in this ministry since its very beginning. And I continue to support it. I consider it a real privilege to endorse this work. Thank God for Teen Challenge!"

—REV. BILLY GRAHAM

"In reading Don Wilkerson's new book, *First Step*, I am convinced that it will benefit pastors, addicts and anyone who wishes to be involved in remedying the downward-spiraling drug epidemic! It is full of wisdom, bringing the God-factor to the forefront as The Remedy to the problem. The author has spent 54 years working with Teen Challenge, helping to rehabilitate thousands of addicts. He knows firsthand what works!"

—JESSE OWENS, FOUNDER, GLOBAL RENEWAL, INC.

"Having known Pastor Don for over twenty years, I can say that his kindness, his his commitment to seeing lives od has never wavered. To read th him over a good, hot meal where he'll tell you the truth, with genuine fatherly love."

—PASTOR CHARLES SIMPSON, ASSOCIATE PASTOR, PILLARS OF FAITH, QUEENS, NY

"I appreciate Don Wilkerson's writing style. It is laid out in a way that is easily understood by someone with an addiction or life-controlling issue. The advice is to be taken as much more than advice. This is wisdom!"

—**MARIAH N. FREEMAN**, GRADUATE OF THE WALTER HOVING HOME, A TEEN CHALLENGE PROGRAM

"The Teen Challenge program succeeds when all of the government programs have failed."

—**CHARLES COLSON**, PRISON FELLOWSHIP

"The ministry and dedication of Teen Challenge deserve the commendation of every citizen."

—**PRESIDENT RONALD REAGAN**

"A government funded research project concluded that Teen Challenge has the highest success rate in helping people move from substance abuse, off substance abuse."

—**JOHN ASHCROFT**, FORMER U.S. SENATOR AND FORMER U.S. ATTORNEY GENERAL

YOUR
FIRST
STEP TO
Freedom

Dan Wilbur

YOUR FIRST STEP TO *Freedom*

DON WILKERSON

BL BRIDGE LOGOS

Newberry, FL 32669

Bridge-Logos, Inc.
Newberry, FL 32669

Your First Step To Freedom:
Beginning the Journey to Finding Freedom
by Don Wilkerson

Printed in the United States of America

Library of Congress Catalog Card Number: 2018949512

International Standard Book Number: 978-1610362146

Cover/Interior design by Kent Jensen | knail.com

*Minor misprint in the upper left-hand corner of the pages - wrong title.

CONTENTS

Part One: THE FIRST STEP 1

1. Introducing the First Step Toward Freedom 3
2. The Slippery Slope 9
3. A Personal Message for the Addict
   or Substance Abuser 17
4. Others Have Taken the First Step, and So Can You ... 26
5. The Purpose of Prayer 39
6. The Power of a Simple Prayer. 48

Part Two: YOUR NEXT STEPS 61

7. Your Next Two Vital Steps 62
8. How to Avoid a Relapse. 71

Part Three: FIRST STEPS FOR INTERVENERS 91

9. Steps Toward Intervention 92
10. From Denial to Decision 109
11. Developing a First Step Prayer Team. 116

The Mission of Teen Challenge 131

Part One

THE FIRST STEP

Chapter One

INTRODUCING THE FIRST STEP TOWARD FREEDOM

"That's one small step for man, one giant leap for mankind."

—NEIL ARMSTRONG

The above quote was from the first man to step onto the moon. Only a few have ever made that incredible step in outer space. Another challenge awaits millions here on planet earth—how to take the FIRST STEP to conquering the inner spaces of the heart and mind that are captivated by potential life-destroying habits.

If you or a loved one have a serious life-controlling problem, what is the first and most important step that needs to be taken to begin the journey toward freedom from that problem?

There is no magical, one-step solution to freedom from such problems as drug addiction, alcoholism, pornography, or addiction to gambling or sex. But all journeys begin with a FIRST STEP. Since there is so much at stake when dealing with a life-controlling problem, getting started on the right step is vital to achieving success. The right FIRST STEP can launch you or your loved one on a journey to freedom from habits that are harmful or lead to addictions that can be destructive and even life-threatening.

> All journeys begin with a FIRST STEP.
> Getting started on the right step is vital to
> achieving success.

Do you (or does your loved one) need to enter a short- or long-term residential rehabilitation program? Will an outpatient program help? What about Alcoholics Anonymous (AA) and similar Twelve-Step Programs? These are all possible options to consider if the person is ready and willing to seek help.

FIRST STEP is not really a "program." It is, however, a challenge to addicts or about-to-be-addicts that can help them to begin to go in the right direction even prior to making a commitment to one type of program or another.

The challenge laid out in this book is actually one that most programs for addicts completely ignore—that is, addressing people's spiritual needs along with their psychological, physiological, and emotional needs. For example, many Twelve-Step Programs begin with acknowledging the significance of a higher power, yet do so in such a vague manner that most who participate in the program fail to take this step seriously. In doing so, they bypass the most important step of all in getting freed from alcoholism (or whatever the person's addiction may be).

FIRST STEP is about two persons, the Person of God and the person with the addiction problem. When these two persons connect, really connect, great things happen! The thing that establishes the connection is prayer. There is no greater power on earth than simple, but heartfelt prayer from a sincere prayer.

> There is no greater power on earth than simple, but heartfelt prayer from a sincere pray-er.

What amazes me is how some "faith-based" rehab programs do not understand the importance of FIRST STEP prayers. Even those that are advocates of the Twelve-Step Program rarely actually pray at a meeting or encourage private prayers. It's like having a cure for some sickness sitting in a filled prescription bottle in your medicine cabinet and never taking it. The God who spoke the world into existence is available to all who will seek Him. He will come and make Himself known and display His power to all who need freedom from destructive powers in their lives.

I purposely wrote *First Step* for those who know in their heart of hearts that they need help, but have, thus far, been unwilling to do anything about it. Perhaps they are too proud or too fearful, or they have never heard that they can be free of their problem by raising their hands to God and asking for His supernatural help.

Many who have a life-controlling problem are afraid to admit it because they are fearful of putting themselves in the hands of others they do not trust. So, the easiest thing to do is to deny the problem in order to avoid having to follow someone's directions to do this or that to get the help they need.

What some addicts do to get loved ones off their back is make all kinds of attempted beginnings to get help, but never follow through to a "happy ending" that results in complete freedom from addiction. Or, to put it another way, they take all kinds of first steps, maybe even commit to a Twelve-Step Program, but with step *thirteen* they stumble and fall.

There are literally thousands who have taken the FIRST STEP and today are free from a problem that almost kept them from walking at all. Most of these people are unknown to us because they do not want others to know about their past. In some respects, not knowing who these individuals are and how they overcame their problem is unfortunate.

I encourage those of you who made the God connection, and overcame shameful habits and behavior, to be willing to share your story privately with others who demonstrate all the familiar signs of addiction. Because you've been there and done that, your story can help them make the FIRST STEP. I refer especially to the working addict, alcoholic, gambler, or those with other serious addictions. These are the hardest to reach. If you were once one of the unreachable ones who have been changed by the grace of God, then take a bold step and help someone who is where you used to be.

To those dealing with a loved one with a life-controlling problem, you also need to know the FIRST STEP you must take to help you cope with living with or watching a loved one go down the road to their "wits' end." I have included chapters here to help you, too. And, if the reader is someone who has a life-controlling problem, it is no accident that you have this book in your hands. The fact that you're reading this now is a pre-first step so you can learn how your life can be changed.

If you're an admitted addict, or addicted to whatever, and you've tried and failed in a program or even numerous programs, you of all people need to know what was missing in all those other programs. The question I address in one of the chapters is this: *Did you fail the program, or did the program fail you?*

No matter what category you fall into, this book will help you "walk the walk" by learning what the FIRST STEP is, and by taking it for yourself or stepping with a loved one toward freedom from a life-controlling problem.

Chapter Two

THE SLIPPERY SLOPE

"I passed on to you what was most important and what had also been passed on to me."

(1 CORINTHIANS 15:3)

Is it possible to find freedom from the bondage of a severe life-controlling problem such as pornography, sex, gambling, drugs, and/or alcohol?

If so, and if a person desires such freedom, what is the first thing, the very FIRST STEP one must take to enter the Freedom Road to overcoming such a problem?

No one ever starts out to become addicted to certain indulgences. However, what usually begins as a taste can end up as a tragedy. A simple curiosity can eventually become a curse. There is such a powerful lure to experience the forbidden fruit, that a one-time lust can become a once-a-week desire and eventually turn into an irresistible habit, then an addiction.

> What usually begins as a taste can
> end up as a tragedy, and a simple curiosity
> can eventually become a curse.

Every first-timer or occasional user of drugs, whether soft drugs like marijuana or hard drugs such as cocaine or heroin, is a potential long-term drug addict.

Every drinker of moderation is a potential alcoholic. A person who makes too many trips to Las Vegas or the local racetrack, or engages in other forms of gambling frequently or periodically, can be classified as an "addict." The Internet is a daily invitation to a wide assortment of games to feed the gambler's addiction. A computer can also become a window into pornographic sites and may lead to a habitual dependence that distorts a person's sexuality.

An addict! Am I one of them?
Am I in the process of becoming one of them?
Is my loved one or friend one of them?

The hard part, of course, is to first ask these questions and to come to grips with the truth, and to get your loved one to admit to having a problem. This book is for those who think they don't need help, as well as for those who know they do.

What are the programs that can help a person conquer a serious life-controlling problem? Do you, or your loved one, need a traditional "program"? If so, which one? If not, what other options are there?

There's the famous Twelve-Step Program such as Alcoholics Anonymous and other programs similar to AA. There are programs for gamblers, sex addicts, and other types of addictions based on the AA model.

There are short- and long-term treatments offered by hospitals and other private, therapeutic programs. There are outpatient professional, counseling services for those who can afford them.

Some private, hospital-based programs and clinics offer short-term rehabilitation at a cost of approximately $750 a day. Malibu, California, which has twenty-six residential programs, is the center of addiction treatment for celebrities. A thirty-day program can cost from $40,000 to $100,000. Only the rich can afford this type of rehab.

There are faith-based residential programs such as Teen Challenge, Victory Outreach, New Life for Youth, and others.

Are these the only options for a person needing help? Are the only people finding freedom from addiction the ones who enter and complete a traditional treatment program?

Or are people getting set free in other ways that we don't know about? The answer is yes!

There are some former drug abusers and those who were chemically dependent now living free from substance abuse who never went through a long-term, faith-based residential program, or any other type of structured program. I meet them all the time, mostly in churches I visit. Their changed lives came about as a "God thing." In other words, they turned their lives over to God and He turned their lives around.

They went through no traditional treatment program. They had an encounter with God that occurred with the help of people of faith. Whether in a small-group Bible study or attending a church service (or even reading a Christian book such as the one in your hands), they heard the message of hope and deliverance that comes through Jesus Christ, and experienced a miracle that changed their lives.

> There are many former drug abusers
> now living free from substance abuse
> through an encounter with God.

This can happen to you! And it can happen to your loved one or your dear friend.

If you have a serious life-controlling problem and want to quit, how is it possible? What step or steps can you take to come clean?

What is the first and most important step? I'm going to tell you.

I am not talking about entering a "program" to find help. If you think you don't need a program, you may be right. I'm going to show you how you might possibly avoid going into a short- or long-term program.

Perhaps only a select few do not need a "program" and you may be one of them.

I suspect there are many more people than anyone realizes who have escaped from drug and alcohol abuse and other life-controlling problems. But because they wanted to keep their problem private, their recovery was kept private as well. I have been a co-pastor of a large church in New York City and know from experience that there were dozens, if not hundreds, saved from substance abuse directly through the ministry of the church, apart from having gone through any specialized "program." How did they do it? What step or steps did they take to get free?

If you are interested in finding out how you can overcome drug use, abuse, or addiction, or other life-controlling problems, let me introduce you not to a Twelve-Step Program, but a FIRST STEP plan of action. Ultimately, you may need a Twelve-Step Program or even need to go into residential care. But if you feel you're not ready for that, then allow yourself to hear more about the FIRST STEP toward freedom from a life-controlling problem.

I repeat: It is possible to overcome an addiction without taking medication, seeing a psychologist or therapist, going through group therapy such as AA, or entering some private and costly addiction treatment program. Many have found this revolutionary cure, and so can you.

If you're the loved one or friend of someone addicted, then you probably already know that getting that person to commit to some structured "program" is difficult. If this person is not ready for a traditional type of treatment, perhaps taking a FIRST STEP can help them.

The FIRST STEP can be helpful not only for a drug or alcohol abuser, but for someone hooked on pornography, gambling, or sexual addictions. Throughout this book, references will be made primarily to drug addicts and alcoholics. However, the reader can just as well substitute another form of addiction whenever the terms drugs or alcohol are used.

> The FIRST STEP can be helpful for people
> in all types of addictions.

Talking about a FIRST STEP action to overcome destructive habits is not a gimmick. It's not an easy way out—not at all. Finding answers to any of life's problems always begins with understanding the right path to take and then taking that *FIRST STEP*. There are many more steps one must take to live victoriously, but the most important thing is to know what the FIRST STEP is and then be willing to take it. The other steps become easier after the first one is taken.

It's amazingly easy, yet hard at the same time, to take the FIRST STEP. Those who offer treatment for addiction and life-controlling problems sometimes make it too hard. So the person needing help is scared off.

If you are curious about this FIRST STEP for yourself or someone you care about, read on.

Most people who try to triumph over an addiction problem and fail to do so did not take the right FIRST STEP. When you get off on the wrong foot, one bad step leads to another and the person seeking help ends up being disillusioned. Many do fail, even when they have the right program. But just as many fail because they have not sought and found help from the right source.

The Bible says in the book of Jeremiah, *"O LORD, I know the way of man is not in himself; it is not in man who walks to direct his own steps"* (10:23, NKJV).

Another Bible translation of this same verse says, *"We are not able to plan our own course."* How true this is when trying to find freedom from a life-controlling problem. The good news is God has already provided the course, the steps up and out of addiction.

If you think you don't have a drug or alcohol problem, then this is not for you now, but it may be for you later. That is, if you survive when things get out of control. By the time some people realize they need help, they are tragically out of touch with those who can help them, or they are literally out of touch with reality. There is always a line a person crosses from infrequent use of a substance to addiction, but the person never knows when they've crossed that line, and then it's often too late or too difficult to do something about it.

The book of Proverbs contrasts those who follow the path (steps) to freedom with those who foolishly follow the downward steps to an uncertain end. Here is one of those contrasts between the free and the imprisoned:

> *"The way [steps] of the righteous is like the first gleam of dawn, which shines ever brighter until the full light of day. But the way [steps] of the wicked is like total darkness. They have no idea what they are stumbling over."*
>
> (PROVERBS 4:18,19)

> *"But as for me, I almost lost my footing. My feet were slipping, and I was almost gone."*
>
> (PSALM 73:2)

How close are you to slipping into addiction?
It's a slippery slope!
Don't let this happen to you.

Chapter Three

A PERSONAL MESSAGE FOR THE ADDICT OR SUBSTANCE ABUSER

This chapter is for you if you're an addict or if your loved ones "think" you have an addiction problem, but you don't think you do. You don't have to read every chapter in this book if you don't want to. But, please, read this one—if not for your sake, then at least for the sake of your mother, father, spouse, friend, or whoever put this book into your hand.

Remember, I am not trying to persuade you to go into a "program." I'm asking you to acquire some helpful knowledge and information. You can ignore it, but who knows? Some of what you read may prove to be very helpful to you.

> What you read here may prove
> to be very helpful to you.

First, let me make this point: It does not matter to me if you're a casual drug user, weekend drinker, or habitual user. It's immaterial whether you have a big habit, little habit, or no habit at all at this point. The fact that you are any kind of drug or alcohol user (or have another type of life-controlling problem) places you at risk. Just look around at some of your friends who are users, maybe even addicts. They can tell you a lot about where you *may* be headed.

Do you know a user who is in prison? Do you know someone who has needed medical treatment or hospitalization for detox, or worse, had an overdose? Have you or a friend ever lost control once, twice, even many times because of drinking excessively? Do you know anyone who has hepatitis or is HIV-positive because of intravenous drug abuse? If you don't, there are thousands of them out there, and they're a lot closer to you than you think.

If none of this has happened to you, you can thank God. The fact that it's happened to some of your friends at least shows you what kind of people you hang out with. "At-risk" people almost always go too far and do the wrong things and get themselves into trouble. Be honest. That's what drugs and alcohol are doing to you. But then again, you're different, aren't you?

Or are you?

How can you be sure?

At this point in your substance abuse, or your gambling, sexual, or pornography addiction, you may feel lucky not to be worse off. I prefer to call it the grace of God. You're living on borrowed time. Any day now may be payday and the wages can be frightening.

Admit it: You have entered a world filled with dangerous minefields and your behavior can at any moment blow up in your face. If you minimize your habit, you will not maximize the opportunity to get help.

> If you minimize your habit, you will not maximize the opportunity to get help.

If you're a frequent or even infrequent pot-smoker or a heavy drinker and rationalize your substance use by saying things like, "Everyone gets high once in a while," you may rationalize yourself right into serious addiction.

The challenge to you is this: Are you willing and ready to stop, and to stop forever? Until that decision is made, no book you read, no one trying to reach out and help you, no Scripture or prayer on your behalf is going to work. You have the power of choice. We make our choices and our choices turn around and make us, for better or worse.

Don't take the risk of joining Elvis Presley, Marilyn Monroe, Bruce Lee, River Phoenix, Anna Nichole Smith, Amy Winehouse, Heath Ledger, Michael Jackson, and thousands of others who passed on before their time. The list of famous and not-so-famous people who have died as the result of too much drugs or alcohol is long, very long. Don't add your name to that list!

The addiction clock is ticking. Don't let it strike twelve, the "lights out" hour.

What's your decision?

I have known many hardcore addicts and alcoholics who would have given anything to have someone intervene in their situation as they were on the road to devastation, and stop them before they reached dead-end street. You may be at a point where your downward spiral can be stopped. There is an exit ramp off your broad road to destruction. You just need to know it and take it, once you see the sign. I am holding up the sign to you right now. Probably others have, as well.

> There is an exit ramp off your broad road to destruction, and I am holding up the sign to you right now.

You can be wise, or you can be a fool.

Wise people stop and think! Fools ignore the warnings and go on.

The Bible has some very relevant Scriptures to address this. There are some amazing words of warning and promises aimed right at your heart and your situation found within the Word of God. Here are a few of these words of wisdom:

"Fools think their own way is right, but the wise listen to others."

(PROVERBS 12:15)

"Wisdom will multiply your days and add years to your life. If you become wise, you will be the one to benefit. If you scorn wisdom, you will be the one to suffer."

(PROVERBS 9:11,12)

"Walk with the wise and become wise; associate with fools and get in trouble."

(PROVERBS 13:20)

Where are you walking? And who are you walking with: the wise or the foolish?

If you want to wise up, then read on.

THE TOP TEN LIST OF MISERIES FROM SUBSTANCE ABUSE

(from Proverbs 23:29–35)

1. *"Who has anguish?"*
2. *"Who has sorrow?"*
3. *"Who is always fighting?"*
4. *"Who is always complaining?"*
5. *"Who has unnecessary bruises?"*
6. *"Who has bloodshot eyes?"*
7. *"You will see hallucinations, and you will say crazy things."*
8. *"You will stagger like a sailor tossed at sea."*
9. *"And you will say, 'They hit me, but I didn't feel it. I didn't even know it when they beat me up.'"*
10. *"When will I wake up so I can look for another drink?"*

You may say, "But those things haven't happened to me."

Good! You're fortunate. However, can you be sure that tomorrow one or more of the above descriptions of a life out of control will not happen to you? You may be in charge now, but you are taking in a substance that, for millions of people, slowly but surely demands a little more. And then it requires more frequent intake, and finally you are no longer in charge. You can become a prisoner to a pleasure that becomes a poison.

> You can become a prisoner to a pleasure
> that becomes a poison.

The same Bible passage that describes the drunkard and alcoholic above says this: *"Don't gaze at the wine, seeing how red it is, how it sparkles in the cup, how smoothly it goes down. For in the end it bites like a poisonous snake; it stings like a viper"* (Proverbs 23:31,32). You can substitute the word "wine" and put in your drug of choice, and the same thing can result. Snakes and vipers bite whom they want to, and there is no way you can control them.

You can call yourself a casual user, a moderate drinker, a light gambler, an Internet user, or whatever term to downgrade your conduct, but the very fact that you're reading this should tell you something.

Adam Harbinson writes:

The jails, prisons, hospitals, and graveyards are full of people who thought they weren't addicts. I read literature about persons who use, but say they were not addicted... until they crossed an invisible line to being an addict. Problem is I never found anyone who could tell me or describe what or where that line is.

(GOD & ALCOHOL DON'T MIX)

Take the FIRST STEP before you stumble and fall. Take the FIRST STEP to stop before you are powerless to quit. Learn from the experiences and tragedies of others. No one sets out to become an addict, an alcoholic, or a slave to sexual activities. It happens to those who thought they were smarter than others.

Take the FIRST STEP toward abstinence and sobriety before some of the following things happen to you. The Bible talks about those who found help, but before they did, they experienced some of the things listed below (from Psalm 107). Believe me, you don't want these things to happen to you.

1. *"Some wandered...lost and homeless"* (v. 4).
2. *"Hungry and thirsty, they nearly died"* (v. 5).
3. *"Some sat in darkness and deepest gloom, imprisoned in iron chains of misery"* (v. 10).
4. *"[They experienced] hard labor; they fell, and no one was there to help them"* (v. 12).
5. *"Some were fools; they rebelled and suffered for their sins"* (v. 17).
6. *"They couldn't stand the thought of food, and they were knocking on death's door"* (v. 18).
7. *"They reeled and staggered like drunkards and were at their wits' end"* (v. 27).

Don't end up at "wits' end." Wits have to do with intelligence, or street smarts. In other words, you can think you are smarter than those who experienced the things listed above, but you can be outsmarted and end up on a dead-end street with no way to get yourself out of trouble. That street is called Wits' End.

There is good news, however!

You can take the FIRST STEP off the road you are on. The Bible says these same people described above in Psalm 107 did something about their situation. They took the FIRST STEP that brought them out of their hopeless plight into a brand new way of life and living. They cried out to the Lord God. This can happen to you, as well. Read on!

> *"'LORD, help!' they cried in their trouble, and he rescued them from their distress."*
>
> (PSALM 107:6,13,19,28)

Are you ready to take this step to freedom?

Chapter Four

OTHERS HAVE TAKEN THE FIRST STEP, AND SO CAN YOU

Let's suppose you have made the wise decision to seek help. What then should you do?

I'm assuming you either believe God is the One who ultimately will help you change, or at least you're open to getting to know Him. How then can you learn about God's way of recovery and healing?

The answer begins with turning yourself over to God.

Many drug users and addicts say they recognize that it takes "will power" to change. Yes, you have to *want* to change and be *willing* to change before you can. But many do not know they can change. Yes, it takes your "will" and desire to live clean, but merely wanting to do something is different from having the strength and power to actually do it.

This is where God comes in.

> Merely wanting to do something is different from having the strength to actually do it. This is where God comes in.

Your *will* and God's *power* need to come together and work together to bring about the real and lasting change that you need.

The most important thing for you to know in order to change is this: You can change! You can be set free! You really can have a new beginning, a brand new life! I know this because I have seen the evidence in thousands of lives transformed from all types of addictions.

> You really can have a brand new life! I know this because I have seen the evidence in thousands of lives.

It all starts with God! In order for you to receive His help, you will need to understand three simple truths:

- God is *willing* to change you!
- God is *able* to change you!
- God is *ready* to change you!

Let's examine these three statements.

(Remember, I am assuming that you have the will, the desire, and the want-to to seek help from God. If you're an agnostic or a stubborn unbeliever, then you either need to find another way to get help, or you might have to get worse off before becoming desperate enough to at least try God and His way.)

GOD IS *WILLING* TO CHANGE YOU

There is a wonderful story in the Bible in the New Testament about a man, a leper, who came to Jesus. His story is important for two reasons. One, God does His work through Jesus Christ. Two, Jesus is God who came in the flesh. Jesus is alive now, and what He did when He was on earth, He is still doing today.

> Jesus is alive now, and what He did when He was on earth, He is still doing today.

This leper was much like the addicts of today. He had an incurable disease. He was an outcast. In those days, if a leper was walking down a road and saw someone approaching, he had to holler out loud, "Unclean, unclean," so the other person would know to pass on the other side and avoid any contact with him. The leper who came to Jesus was desperate for help. He cried out to Him, saying, *"If you are willing, you can heal me and make me clean"* (Mark 1:40).

Jesus then touched the man and said, *"I am willing. Be healed!"* (Mark 1:41).

It's amazing that Jesus actually touched this leper. A religious Jew in those days was not permitted to touch lepers. Jesus could have said, "I am willing to heal you, but don't come close to me." Instead, Jesus touched him, and in so doing, not only healed the man's physical wounds, but also his emotional hurts from living in isolation and rejection. Your case is just like this leper, in that Jesus wants to heal you. He is willing, and you need to believe this.

Even if you have some doubts about God and Jesus, it does not change the fact that God is willing to restore you to the person you were before the drugs, the drinking, or other destructive activities. I highlighted "even if" because I would like to answer some of your "even ifs" that you may have about whether God is willing to help you.

Even if you were brought up in a Christian or religious home and you drifted away from Christianity, you can come back to those roots and discover a personal relationship with God through Jesus Christ. When you left God, He never left you.

Even if you were hurt by some Christian (or so-called Christian) and are bitter toward God, He understands. God does not like what was done to you any more than you do. I'm not offering you Christians. I am offering you Christ!

You may have other "even ifs" such as doubts, fears, confusion, guilt, and loads of questions about God and His willingness to come to you and make right the things that are wrong.

Your FIRST STEP then is to believe that God is the Source from where your help comes. The Bible says, *"It is impossible to please God without faith. Anyone who wants to come to him must believe that God exists and that he rewards those who sincerely seek him"* (Hebrews 11:6).

Do you want the "reward" that comes from believing God? You can experience the reward if you come to Him with an open, believing heart. The basic thing to believe is that God is willing to come to your aid.

A fellow named Ken did just this. His mother was a drug addict and he became one as well. One night he overdosed on a synthetic opiate called DXM. He'd ingested 1½ grams of the drug and his brain slowly began to shut off. Ken was unable to stand up, speak coherently, see straight, or even remember his name. Then he sobered up enough to say a prayer.

His words went like this: "God...I don't know if I have broken something [in my head], but I know that ultimately You are in control. And I would like You to take control of my life."

God did answer Ken's prayer. He says, "Not only has my brain fully recovered from the overdose, but I thank God daily for this second chance at life that He has given me."

What God did for Ken, He can do for you. Just ask Him!

GOD IS *ABLE* TO CHANGE YOU

Some people believe God is able to perform miracles, but is unwilling to do so for them. Others believe in God, but they do not see Him as being able to change them because they do not know His Word, His ways, and His workings. The leper mentioned earlier apparently knew Jesus was able to heal a leper, probably because he'd heard of other lepers having been healed by Jesus. So his question was, "Was Jesus *willing?*"

God, through His Son Jesus, is not only willing to help and heal you, but He is more than able to, as well. Just check His record in the Bible. Jesus healed lepers, forgave adulterers, took the thief who died next to Him on the cross to heaven with Him, and He did so many other miracles that it would have taken volumes of books to contain the results.

This same miracle-working Jesus is still alive, and the Bible declares that *"Jesus Christ is the same yesterday, today, and forever"* (Hebrews 13:8).

I have worked with hardcore addicts and alcoholics for over fifty years (I started very young), and I have seen thousands healed, cured, and changed for life. Some of them are now successful in work and various businesses. Many are workers in faith-based rehabilitation programs, helping those who are where they once were. Others are ministers, missionaries, community workers, and faithful churchgoers. They live normal lives. Once, society said they were incurable, but now they are living and walking miracles.

And God does not show favoritism (Romans 2:11). This means that what He has done for any other man or woman or youth, He can do for you, too.

> What God has done for any other man or woman or youth, He can do for you, too.

Yes, God is both willing and *able*.

The Bible records a prayer of the great apostle Paul who once called himself the "worst" of sinners (1 Timothy 1:15). In this prayer Paul says, *"I pray that you will understand the incredible greatness of God's power for us who believe him"* (Ephesians 1:19).

A man named Raymond experienced God's power and willingness to help him. Raymond was a cocaine user and dabbled in Satanism. In a seventeen-year period he went through many rehabs, but nothing seemed to fill the void in his life. At one point he stayed clean for about a year and got married. Soon after, however, he made some bad choices and, falling into bad habits, he was back on the stuff. His marriage fell apart.

Raymond says, "At the end, I sold whatever I had left and went to die. I was hiding out so no one could find me. I would do a little work for the dealer and he gave me some drugs and a little food. As I was going through this time, I felt a tugging on my heart. It was like God was telling me that He had something better for me."

God did have something better for Raymond. His sister came and found him. At first, she did not know who he was, telling him he did not seem like her brother any more. She started to cry! A friend of mine, Jesse Owens, had once met her at an airport and told her he was associated with a faith-based rehabilitation program. She remembered this when she finally found her brother, and took him to the program Rev. Owens recommended. It was Teen Challenge.

"The Lord has been good to me," Raymond shares in telling his personal story of recovery and rehabilitation. "The crying on the inside for help has been heard."

Yes, God heard Raymond's cry and He will hear yours, too. The Bible, in the book of Psalms, describes what Raymond experienced. *"In my distress I cried out to the LORD; yes, I prayed to my God for help. He heard me from his sanctuary; my cry to him reached his ears"* (18:6).

Psalm 107 was quoted in a previous chapter regarding the bad things that happen to some people. Well, I left some of the good part out of what happened to these very same people. The Bible says they were "lost" and "nearly died," and "no one was there to help them."

These very same people had this happen to them:

1. *"He rescued them from their distress"* (v. 6).
2. *He filled their appetites "with good things"* (v. 9).
3. *"He saved them from their distress"* (v. 13).
4. *"He...healed them, snatching them from the door of death"* (v. 20).
5. *"He calmed the storm to a whisper and stilled the waves"* (v. 29).

How did this happen? Four times in Psalm 107 it says they cried out in their trouble, "LORD, help!" Every cry for help was met with a positive outcome.

Your cry can reach God's ears, but you have to take the FIRST STEP and pray.

If you have not been willing to change, or if you tried and failed and have given up, you need to know that with God all things are possible (Matthew 19:26). If you haven't wanted to change because you don't believe it's possible, it's time to change your thinking.

> If you haven't wanted to change because you don't believe it's possible, it's time to change your thinking.

Your FIRST STEP toward change may be as simple as realizing that you have been hindered by a lack of knowledge. The Bible is full of hope for you. It is food for your mind and soul. Consider these verses:

"Is anyone thirsty? Come and drink—even if you have no money! Come take your choice of [a new kind of] *wine* [or high] *or milk* [this means Gods' Word]*—it's all free! Why spend your money on food* [and a cure] *that does not give you strength? Why pay for food that does you no good? Listen to me, and you will eat what is good. You will eat the finest food."*

(ISAIAH 55:1,2; AUTHOR'S WORDS IN BRACKETS)

"Come to me [the Lord is saying] *with your ears wide open. Listen, and you will find life. I will make an everlasting covenant* [agreement] *with you. I will give you all the unfailing love* [that you need]*..."*

(ISAIAH 55:3)

"Seek the LORD while you can find him. Call on him now while he is near.... Yes, turn to our God, for he will forgive generously."

(ISAIAH 55:6,7)

"These events will bring great honor to the LORD's name; they will be an everlasting sign of his power and love."

(ISAIAH 55:13)

GOD IS *READY* TO CHANGE YOU

God is not only willing to change your life, He is also able to do it, and He is *ready to do it now*. There is no waiting list or waiting time.

The Bible says, *"Today is the day of salvation"* (2 Corinthians 6:2).

I have seen so many substance abusers admit they need help, but then they procrastinate. They put it off too long. Some are too proud to humble themselves and admit their helplessness. Others could not give up the god they had made of their addiction. Some are serving long-term prison sentences. Some are HIV-positive. Some are dying of AIDS or other diseases. And some have died.

In all things in life we often put off things for another day. It has been said, "You may not have another day. Procrastination is the assassination of motivation."

The devil's favorite tool is tricking people to put things off. Outsmart him. Do it now.

If ever the word "now" applies to someone, it's you. If you play with fire, you might get burned. You're playing a game much more dangerous—it's called Russian roulette. The next hit, bottle, pill, or snort could be your last. Or, you could lose your job (if you still have one), lose your marriage, your children. You have probably already lost your self-respect.

The clock is ticking! Things rarely, if ever, get better for the drug user. Use turns to abuse, abuse to addiction, and addiction turns to…well, you fill in the blank.

Drinking casually and occasionally can turn into a habit, and a habit into alcoholism. The alcoholic's steps down are often slower than the cocaine addict, the meth abuser, or the heroine addict. But the destruction on the way down is so deceptive, yet so terminal, that one day you wake up and you are no longer *you*. You are another person altogether who no longer has it together.

The same results can happen if gambling, pornography, or a promiscuous lifestyle is your addiction. These kinds of habits may be hidden from others, but they are not hidden from God; and you can be quietly living a double life that affects you in more ways than you want to admit.

God is ready *now* to change your heart, mind, and soul and save you from a fate that's even worse than your current state of being.

Listen to more of Raymond's story mentioned earlier. He says, "My family members are amazed at the new me. I myself sometimes get a little scared at the speed in which God can accomplish things in my life. When I look back on my past, it brings tears to my eyes. But when I look forward, it brings joy. I need to ask my son, my daughters, and my wife for forgiveness. The best thing I can do is to forgive and to stay on this path, because He is the way."

God is in the business of changing people, no matter how far wrong they have gone.

He can do it for you!

Will you let Him?

If so, let me tell you what you can do to help make it happen.

Chapter Five

THE PURPOSE OF PRAYER

"I urge you, first of all, to pray for all people. Ask God to help them; intercede on their behalf, and give thanks for them."

(1 TIMOTHY 2:1)

The distance between you and God is just a prayer away. It is the FIRST STEP that needs to be taken to begin the journey toward freedom from any life-destroying problem.

Prayer is something a lot of people believe in, but rarely do; at least they rarely do it the way it should be done.

I want to tell you how you can take the path directly to a cure. There is no shortcut to a lifelong cure, but it begins with the power to change. Prayer connects you to the One with the power. Or, as stated in the previous chapter, prayer is the step you take to connect to a God who is *willing, able, and ready* to help you. It is this mighty power you will need to follow all the other future steps necessary to be changed and to stay changed for the rest of your life.

> Prayer is the step you take to connect to a God who is **willing, able, and ready** to help you.

In the famously successful Twelve-Step Program of AA, steps one, two, and three are as follows:

1. "We admitted we were powerless over alcohol—that our lives had become unmanageable."
2. "We came to believe that a Power greater than ourselves could restore us to sanity."
3. "We made a decision to turn our will and our lives over to the care of God, *as we understood Him.*"

This is good, as far as it goes. But why not go right to *the* Source of Power, Jesus Christ? Why not turn your life over to the care of God, not as you "understand Him," but as the One who has clearly revealed Himself to us through the Bible—just as millions of others have already done?

Too many in the Twelve-Step Program miss the FIRST and most important STEP by allowing others to interpret who this "higher power" is.

The FIRST STEP model that is presented here combines the first three steps of AA into one. Serious, sincere, fervent prayer gets you in touch with the Almighty God who is able to set you free, free forever, from your life-controlling problem. This is not a shortcut, and it does not mean there are not other steps required. But there is a first encounter with God that is so great, so deep, and so powerful that it establishes a foundation upon which you can build and grow strong enough to overcome the temptations that are sure to come.

The FIRST STEP then is to pray a simple, but meaningful prayer, asking God to heal and change you by giving you the power to overcome substance abuse or other practices that are now part of your lifestyle. Don't get hung up on labels: use, abuse, addiction, what does it matter? Even if a person never used any drugs or drank a drop of alcohol, they still need God. The fact is, however, if you're involved in the use of some life-controlling substance or behavior, it makes it all the more urgent for you to take that FIRST STEP prayer.

> If you're involved in the use of some life-controlling substance or behavior, it makes it all the more urgent for you to take that FIRST STEP prayer.

You can avoid a lot of wasted effort and time on the road to recovery and healing if you will understand some simple things about God, and about prayer. God and prayer go together like a man and woman in marriage.

Prayer links you to God. It is like dialing a number on your phone. The ring sounds in heaven and you get God on the line. It's a power line. It's a salvation line, and the line is never busy. You don't get a recording saying, "Call back later or leave a message." All prayers are messages to God and He hears them immediately. God never puts us on hold.

Prayer is also your 911 call; 911 calls are for emergencies. You need to consider that you are in an emergency situation. If you don't think you are in immediate need, then your prayers will be passive and perhaps even meaningless.

God likes real pray-ers. He responds to desperate cries— reality prayers. Prayer is, or should be, a cry for help such as when someone is drowning in water and unable to swim. It's the cry out of a window of someone caught in a fire on the fifth floor, hollering, "Save me!"

> Prayer is a cry for help such as
> when someone is drowning in water,
> or someone caught in a fire on the fifth
> floor, hollering, "Save me!"

Here is what the Bible says about the need for this kind of desperate praying:

- *"I pray with all my heart; answer me, LORD! I will obey your decrees"* (Psalm 119:145).
- *"Morning, noon, and night I cry out in my distress, and the LORD hears my voice"* (Psalm 55:17).
- *"The eyes of the LORD watch over those who do right; his ears are open to their cries for help"* (Psalm 34:15).

This kind of praying will bring you into the presence of God. You can feel His presence. You may or may not get emotional, but it's okay if you do and okay if you don't. But for sure, you will sense that God's Holy Spirit will begin to dwell inside you. A sensation of cleanliness will come upon you. You will feel a weight lifted off you.

The purpose of prayer as a FIRST STEP toward a total cure is this:

1. **To accept Jesus Christ as the higher power who will forgive you for the sins and bad choices you have made.**

The Bible says, *"No one can come to the Father"* except through Jesus Christ (John 14:6). *"He [God] is so rich in kindness and grace that he purchased our freedom with the blood of his Son and forgave our sins"* (Ephesians 1:7).

When Christ was nailed to the cross, our sins were nailed there with Him. You may feel that you've done so many bad things, how could God ever forgive you? The amazing thing is that He will. Salvation is God's gift of grace to all who have messed up their lives and call upon Him for forgiveness. The Bible says, *"For by grace you have been saved through faith, and that not of yourselves; it is the gift of God"* (Ephesians 2:8, NKJV). A gift is not earned. It's freely given. God's gift to us, to you, is His Son Jesus who died so you might be forgiven of all your wrongdoing and sin, and so you can have eternal life.

Prayer also has a second purpose.

2. **To enter into a relationship with Jesus Christ in which He gives you power to overcome the desire, craving, and temptation for the things that have enslaved your life.**

God assures us, *"Anyone who belongs to Christ has become a new person. The old life is gone; a new life has begun!"* (2 Corinthians 5:17). Christ gives you power over all negative powers and influences, so that *"He who is in you is greater than he who is in the world"* (1 John 4:4, NKJV).

Listen to these testimonies from former drug addicts and alcoholics:

- "I discovered that I cannot live my life without Jesus Christ in it. God is restoring relationships with my family and Him."

- "I have learned patience as well as dealing with my anger. With the help of God, He is putting my life back together."
- "I'm learning how to praise and worship the Lord, how to pray and express myself in a godly way. God is restoring my relationships with my children."

Jesus Christ changed these men's and women's lives. These kinds of testimonies can be repeated many times over. This can be your testimony, as well.

God gives His sons and daughters, His children, power to overcome. The apostle Paul writes about this in Ephesians 1:19,20: *"I also pray that you will understand the incredible greatness of God's power for us who believe him. This is the same mighty power that raised Christ from the dead..."* This same power is available for you to tap into!

The third purpose of prayer involves discovering that God has a better plan for you.

3. To surrender your will to God through Jesus Christ in order to follow His will for your life.

This is probably the hardest thing anyone has to do to fully follow the Lord, and thus, fully enjoy His blessings. We like to be masters of our own lives. The third step of Alcoholics Anonymous is this: "We made a decision to turn our will and our lives over to the care of God, as we understood Him." Those last four words, "as we understood Him," can be a cop out. God's directions (also called the *will of God*) can clearly be understood in His Word, the Bible.

Some people only want to understand God up to a point. The point usually has to do with accepting the fact that God requires full surrender to Him, because only then can we receive all the good things He has for us.

One former addict put it this way: "Surrender! I know how to do that. I surrendered everything good and decent in my life to shoot dope. I eventually found out I was the dope. Now I surrender to God in the same way I surrendered to the old life—with everything in me. My burden was too heavy for me to carry, anyway. It was leading me to death. I decided I needed to get out of the driver's seat and let Someone else do the driving. No more dead-end streets for me. I'm on the freedom path now."

A former, heavy Internet user addicted to pornography shares this: "Every night after my wife went to bed I was online feeding my mind with images to satisfy my lust. I'd quit for a week, maybe two. Then, there I was again doing the same thing. I finally realized I was hooked. All the time, I was going to church faithfully and called myself a Christian. Then a visiting preacher gave a sermon about finding total victory in Christ over destructive habits. I went to the altar and got serious with God. I confessed my sin and surrendered myself, once again to Christ, as I had done so when I was a teenager. Now I'm walking in freedom. I still have the urge from time to time to log on to the old websites, but by God's grace I am not doing so. A verse in the Bible that has helped me is 1 Thessalonians 4:4, *'God's will is for you to be holy, so stay away from all sexual sin.'*"

Surrender in warfare means the soldier becomes a captive to his enemy. Surrender to God means He frees you to become the person He created you to be. You give God your will and He gives you His power. This is real *"will-power!"*

> Surrender to God means He frees you
> to become the person He created you to be.
> You give Him your will and He gives you
> His power: real *"will-power!"*

Chapter Six

THE POWER OF A SIMPLE PRAYER

This chapter contains some important and practical suggestions to help you to engage in prayer.

1. **Decide if you want to pray alone, or have others pray for you.**

You actually should do both. If your first real prayer effort is when others pray for you, then make it a practice to also get alone and talk to God. You can get down by your bed on your knees and talk to God, either silently, in a whisper, or in your natural tone of voice. Right now, if you're alone, you can ask God to change your life. If you do this, you will be taking the FIRST STEP into a whole new way of living, thinking, and feeling.

Sometimes it's easier to begin connecting to God if you have Christians—those who really know how to pray—to pray over you and with you. If this happens, don't get alarmed if some of the persons praying speak loudly to God. If you were drowning, wouldn't you holler loudly for help?

> Sometimes it's easier to begin connecting to God if you have Christians—those who really know how to pray—to pray over you and with you.

Prayer is a humbling thing. It's meant to be that way. Pride has kept many a person back from going to a church altar to be prayed for. It has kept others from even doing it in private.

There was a time in Spirit-filled churches when a person with serious bondages in their life was encouraged to remain at the altar until the one prayed over had a spiritual "breakthrough." This meant there was such an encounter with God and the power of the Holy Spirit that a miracle took place similar to what happened in Jesus' day when the sick or lame were made whole. Many former drug addicts, alcoholics, and others with serious, life-controlling problems can testify that this has happened to them through prayer.

Maybe in your FIRST STEP in this matter of praying to God you'd prefer to be alone—and that's okay. Luke 9:18 says, *"One day Jesus left the crowds to pray alone."*

2. It's good to talk out loud to God when you pray.

Song of Solomon 2:14 says, *"Let me hear your voice."* God hears silent prayers, but it will benefit you more if you actually say words out loud to Him. It's a sign of your need, a way of expressing need. If you go to the store and ask a clerk for something you want to buy, you don't ask the clerk to read your mind. God can read your thoughts, but if you can converse with a stranger, surely you can tell God what you want from Him.

Hearing your own prayers out loud helps you because you are expressing your feelings and emotions to God. This is a good thing. The Bible uses the words "call" and "cry" a lot when it refers to prayer.

You don't need to pray with fancy, religious-sounding words. Be honest and tell Jesus all about what's going on in your head. He knows anyway, but you need to talk it out with Him. His ears are always open to hear your prayers, and He really does answer. Tell Him you are sorry for putting Him off for so long. Tell Him you're fed up with your sins. Tell Him you need Him and want Him, and that you're ready to let Him take over your life and be your guide from now on.

If you do this, you will be praying exactly the way many did in Bible days, as you can read from these verses:

"The ropes of death entangled me; floods of destruction swept over me. The grave wrapped its ropes around me;

death laid a trap in my path. But in my distress I cried out to the LORD; yes, I prayed to my God for help. He heard me..."

(PSALM 18:4–6)

Others prayed very short prayers and got immediate answers:

- *"O God, be merciful to me, for I am a sinner"* (Luke 18:13). This was prayed by a notorious sinner, a crooked tax collector.
- *"Save me, Lord!"* (Matthew 14:30). A prayer of Peter, a disciple of Jesus, who was literally about to drown.
- *"Lord,...have mercy on me! My daughter is demon-possessed and suffering terribly"* (Matthew 15:22, NIV). A heathen woman's desperate prayer.

Here is an example (we call it a testimony) of someone who was desperate enough to be set free from a hardcore addiction that he prayed out loud to God.

The excerpt is from a book entitled *God's Turf* (now out of print). In it is the story of how the converted gang leader Nicky Cruz introduced a heroin addict, Johnny Melendez, to Christ and to the power of prayer:

Nicky took him into the office and began to tell him about God and Jesus Christ. Johnny interrupted, "I've got my own philosophy about Christ. I used to see big signs in the subway saying 'Christ died for our sins.' If he did, I figure I can sin all I want." Nicky showed him in the Bible that he was wrong.

Then he told Johnny to kneel down to pray. "He was praying real loud and it bothered me," Johnny said later. "I wasn't used to it. Nicky was saying, 'God, take away the desire for drugs, the desire for marijuana, the desire for liquor,' and things like that. I was there doing nothing and I was getting sicker because I couldn't get a shot of dope that night. Then [Nicky] grabbed me by the arm and said, 'Johnny, if you really want help, you have to ask God yourself. You have to ask God to change your life and take away your habits.'" Johnny says, "Then something in me began to cry out to God. It wasn't a beautiful prayer. I simply asked God to come to me and to give me a completely new life. As I was praying, it seemed that there was something going on within me...I was feeling good; [like] there was nothing wrong with me."

This was the beginning of a new life for Johnny Melendez. He eventually became a United States Army Chaplain, now retired after serving with honors, as well as being in the Gulf War.

It all started with crying out to God in prayer.

3. **Don't be afraid if you feel God's power come on you when you pray.**

The prophet Isaiah says, *"Lift up your voice with strength, lift it up, be not afraid"* (Isaiah 40:9, NKJV).

God's power on someone can cause a person to weep, to cry, or to perhaps even groan. And in a short time frame you may even begin to feel very happy. Some people call this the "touch of God." It's an inner sense, often called "the witness of the Spirit," the presence and power of God entering your mind, heart, and soul. Don't be afraid if you feel sensations, emotions, and strong feelings welling up inside you. This frequently happens to people when they are entering into God's presence.

Also, don't be disappointed if you don't have strong emotions during or after prayer. After all, prayer is an act of faith. Faith believes God hears you when you pray, even though you may not hear angels singing or have goose bumps or other sensations. Just because someone else may get emotional during prayer, this does not mean it should happen to you. We are all made different, and God does not hear us on the basis of how loud or emotionally we pray, but whether it comes from a sincere heart or not.

One of the signs that God has heard your prayer is that you will have a sense of peace and the feeling that a great burden has been lifted from you. For some, when they realize this, they get very emotional. Others may show little or no outward emotion, but still they have that inward peace. Paul, the great writer of many letters in the Bible, wrote about this wonderful peace that you too can experience: *"Don't worry about anything; instead, pray about everything. Tell God what you need, and thank him for all he has done. Then you will experience God's peace, which exceeds anything we can understand. His peace will guard your hearts and minds as you live in Christ Jesus"* (Philippians 4:6,7).

4. Pray with faith.

Having faith in God when we pray is essential in obtaining the answer. The FIRST STEP is a step of faith, expressed through prayer. These are not two steps, but one. To pray without believing that God is willing, able, and ready to answer is to just be saying meaningless words.

One fellow said to me, "I find it hard to pray, because I have a problem with God."

"And what is that problem?" I asked him.

"Why did God allow this [addiction problem] to happen to me in the first place?"

I answered him this way: "God created us with a free will. He has given you free choice. It was never God's will for you to mess up your life by taking drugs. We make our choices, and then our choices turn around and make us, for better or worse. You chose the lifestyle you are in. Don't put that responsibility or blame on God. If God could or would stop us from doing what we want to do, we would be robots and not human beings with intelligence, personality, and individualism. When God made man, He took a risk by giving him free choice."

> We make our choices, and then
> our choices turn around and make us,
> for better or worse.

He looked at me and said nothing, so I continued.

"God was always available to you to help you. If you had chosen to accept Christ and followed His teaching, you would have never wanted to take drugs in the first place. The good news is that God is ready and waiting for you to take this FIRST STEP toward Him now. It's never too late, and I invite you to do this."

This invitation is for you, as well.

A key verse of Scripture worth repeating says, *"For it is by grace you have been saved, through faith—and this is not from yourselves, it is the gift of God—not by works"* (Ephesians 2:8, NIV).

For the first-stepper, faith is the open hand. It's like in a relay race where the opened hand waits for the baton to be passed before going to the finish line. What a wonderful gift to be handed—the gift of salvation and a new life!

A well-known Christian teacher spoke on a certain occasion and afterward had a question-and-answer time with the audience. After various questions were answered, finally a young man in a wheelchair spoke up. "Sir, I, I want to ask you why did God allow this to happen to me?" He spoke with a stuttering voice.

"Young man, I don't have an answer to that question," the teacher said. "But let me ask you this. If you were not in your physical condition, would you have come to hear a Christian teacher speak about Jesus Christ?"

"No—I doubt it!" was his answer.

Our problems turn us toward someone or something that can help us. This may be why you are reading this book. Would you be reading it if you were a successful businessman or woman with no life-controlling problem such as drugs or alcohol, or whatever the problem? Like the young man, I think I can answer for you: "I doubt it."

> Our problems turn us toward someone
> or something that can help us.

You are at a crossroads. You can go forward toward help, or you can stay on the path you're on. Do you think that path is going to lead you to a better life, or to danger and possibly even death? You make the choice. God gives you the choice.

God wants you to choose Him and His way.

Now is the time to take the FIRST STEP.

You take it by praying—and praying in faith.

Having faith means coming to God with an attitude that He hears you when you pray. One thing that can help is to understand that God is a Father to those who trust in Him. Jesus taught His followers, called disciples, to pray a certain way, that is, to address Him as "Our Father." Jesus said, *"Pray like this: Our Father in heaven, may your name be kept holy"* (Matthew 6:9). The first recorded sentence Jesus uttered included the word "Father" (Luke 2:49). His closing words on the cross began with, "Father." In John's Gospel, Jesus calls God "Father" 140 times!

Martin Luther, who sparked the Great Reformation of the Church, wrote about Christ's prayer, called "The Lord's Prayer":

> *How should we address God? Calling Him Father is a friendly affectionate, deep, and heartfelt way to address Him. For the name Father is instinctive and naturally affectionate. This is why hearing us call Him Father pleases God the most and moves Him to listen to us. By doing so, we acknowledge ourselves as children of God, which again stirs God's heart. There is no voice more dear to a Father than his own child's voice.*

Jesus also said that if earthly fathers desire to give good things to their children, then our Father in heaven even more so wants to give good gifts to His children (Matthew 7:11). When you pray, know that you are not asking Someone who has a clenched fist, so that we have to beg and beg for what we want from Him. God the Father has an open hand, waiting to be asked for what we need.

> *"The LORD is like a father to his children, tender and compassionate to those who fear him."*
>
> (PSALM 103:13)

The Bible is full of promises from God to inspire us when we pray. Here are a few of these promises. Reading them over and over again will encourage you to pray.

- *"You parents—if your children ask for a loaf of bread, do you give them a stone instead? Or if they ask for a fish, do you give them a snake? Of course not! So if you sinful people know how to give good gifts to your children, how much more will your heavenly Father give good gifts to those who ask him"* (Matthew 7:9–11).
- *"When you [referring to God] open your hand, you satisfy the hunger and thirst of every living thing"* (Psalm 145:16). Prayer opens God's hand.
- *"Listen! The LORD's arm is not too weak to save you, nor is his ear too deaf to hear you call"* (Isaiah 59:1).

5. **One more important word about prayer: Pray with desperation.**

When you take the FIRST STEP to ask God to change your life, do it as if you were a drowning man or woman. If you are not desperate for help, you will be like someone trying to decide what kind of sandwich to order for lunch. The FIRST STEP of prayer for freedom from drugs is not for the timid. Praying to God to stop living a life of addiction, whatever it may be, works only when it comes from deep inside you like the cry of a person knowing there is no other way out.

Here are the kinds of prayers a desperate person prays:

- *"In my distress I cried to the LORD; yes, I prayed to my God for help. He heard me from his sanctuary; my cry to him reached his ears."* (Psalm 18:6)
- *"O LORD my God, I cried to you for help, and you restored my health. You brought me up from the grave, O LORD. You kept me from falling into the pit of death."* (Psalm 30:2,3)
- *"I cry out to God; yes, I shout. Oh, that God would listen to me! When I was in deep trouble, I searched for the Lord. All night long I prayed, with hands lifted toward heaven."* (Psalm 77:1,2)

Even before you go on reading, you can stop and take this next moment to pray. Why not right now make your first FIRST STEP prayer?

Here is a suggested prayer:

God, I come to You today. I put my trust in Your Son, Jesus Christ, as my Savior. Although it's hard to comprehend that Your love for me is so great, I believe You gave Your life as a sacrifice so that I might have eternal life. I believe You will give me power and strength to live each day in this new life. I ask You to forgive me for not living Your way. I ask for Your help to become all that You created me to be.

Thank You for coming into my life and giving me Your Holy Spirit. Let all the death inside me be overcome by the power of Your presence. This day I make the decision to turn my life over to You and I will follow in the steps You have written in Your Word.

Thank You for hearing and answering me, in Jesus' name. Amen!

Part Two

YOUR NEXT STEPS

Chapter Seven

YOUR NEXT TWO VITAL STEPS

What steps need to be taken after taking the FIRST STEP?

All who turn their life over to God to manage must learn that following Christ is a lifestyle—the journey of a long-distance runner. To use Olympic terms, being a Christian is not a 100-meter dash. It's a lifetime commitment. Eugene Peterson, author of the popular paraphrase of the Bible in modern language entitled *The Message*, authored another book whose title describes what it means to follow Christ. It's called *A Long Obedience in the Same Direction*. This is what the Christian life requires.

My purpose here is not to go in-depth regarding all the next steps you should take to maintain a life of sobriety and freedom from addiction. However, it's important to emphasize that the FIRST STEP is just the beginning. To use the AA expression of taking "one day at a time," we can also say living free takes one step at a time. With every step forward, you will be creating a distance between what you once were and what you are becoming.

Finding freedom from a life-controlling problem begins with the power encounter with Christ described in the previous chapter. It is called by many names: being saved, being born again, conversion, and being transformed. This is the initial FIRST STEP, but it is a step on a lifelong journey, not a once-done experience in which you now live happily ever after. There must be as strong a desire to take the next steps as there is in taking the first one. The Christian life is much more than a Twelve-Step Program. It's tens of thousands of steps, and some are very hard; some are not so hard. However, there is a great deal of difference between taking steps in the dark, and taking them in the light.

There are two essential steps for progressing down the road to freedom from a life-controlling problem.

The Bible is the roadmap to success for everyone, but especially for those who once were so lost and so blind. *"Your word is a lamp to guide my feet and a light for my path"* (Psalm 119:105). Consider the Bible your daily fix.

It's essential then that you begin reading the Bible. It is daily "light" to show you the way. As long as you walk in the light, you will not walk back into the dark. It's that simple! I mean, it's simple to understand, but not simple to do. But with God's Word inside you, the path you need to follow is doable. Psalm 37:31 says when you fill your heart with God's law, you *"will never slip from his path."*

"I will walk in freedom, for I have devoted myself to your commandments"

(PSALM 119:45).

Read Psalm 119 in its entirety. It's a long one with 176 verses, mostly about the importance of God's Word. Verse 133 says, *"Guide my steps by your word, so I will not be overcome by evil."* Psalm 119:35 says, *"Direct me in the path of your commands, for there I find delight"* (NIV). We might add that we also find success, as well as delight.

When we follow God's path, there are good times and tough times, especially for someone trying to overcome addiction or other serious, life-controlling problems. The more steps you take, the stronger you get. Any runner can tell you that a day's run is the success for the next running challenge they take on. As in the physical, so it is in the spiritual realm! The more you walk in the light of God's Word and the teachings of Jesus Christ, the more faith you develop to walk the walk.

> The more you walk in the light of God's Word, the more faith you develop to walk the walk.

Here are some more of God's promises for faith walkers:

- *"You have made a wide path for my feet to keep them from slipping"* (Psalm 18:36).
- *"You chart the path ahead of me..."* (Psalm 139:3, TLB).
- *"For you have rescued me from death; you have kept my feet from slipping. So now I can walk in your presence, O God, in your life-giving light"* (Psalm 56:13). Those who claim this promise have what we might call "happy feet."
- *"God's...gracious Word can make you into what he wants you to be and give you everything you could possibly need"* (Acts 20:32, The Message).

Another way to keep your steps going further and further away from the old life is by making new connections.

I recall speaking in a church and a young man who'd recently become a Christian asked me to pray for him.

I asked, "What can I pray with you about?"

He said, "I'm not sure. I'm a brand new Christian, but there seems to be something missing in this new life I've received Christ. I was an alcoholic, but now I'm sober and clean. I know God did this for me. I could never have done it on my own."

I asked him if he had a prayer partner or someone else he could talk with. He told me he did not, as he was new in the church and didn't know many people there. I immediately saw what was "missing" for him. I asked if he drank alone in the past, or with others. He said he always drank at a bar. I then asked if he drank at the same bar all the time. He seemed perplexed by my question, but he did say that, yes, he frequented the same bar.

I said, "Look, you are missing the camaraderie (fellowship) you had at the bar. You can't go back to the bar and hang out with old friends. Come on—let me introduce you to the family of God." I took him to some brothers in the church and told them the situation. This man had quit drinking, but he hadn't replaced the fellowship of the bar room atmosphere. He needed to join a small-group Bible study in the church and find new friends and new fellowship. In other words, he needed to make new connections.

This is what the local church is, or should be. It's a place to replace the old with the new. New friends! New fellowship! The new wine of the Spirit! New music! A brand new family!

Rick Warren writes in *The Purpose Driven Life*:

You are called to belong, not just believe...While your relationship to Christ is personal, God never intends it to be private. In God's family you are connected to every other believer, and we will belong to each other for eternity...The Bible says a Christian without a church home is like an organ without a body, a sheep without a flock, or a child

without a family. It is an unnatural state. The Bible says,
"You belong in God's household with every other Christian"
(Ephesians 2:19b, NIV).

It is crucial for all believers to be a part of a specific local church. It is even more indispensable for someone with a life-controlling problem to identify with, and be a part of, some church. You may have to attend a number of different churches until one meets your needs. Usually new Christians are introduced to Christ by friends and loved ones who are already a part of a local church, so this does not necessarily have to be a difficult search. For those who do not know anyone connected to a church, find one that is evangelical, which basically means they teach the biblical truth that salvation comes though faith in Jesus Christ alone.

Here is another excellent quote from Rick Warren:

To Paul, being a "member" of the church meant being a vital organ of a living body, an indispensable, interconnected part of the Body of Christ. We need to recover and practice the biblical meaning of membership. The church is a body, not a building; an organism, not an organization.

One more step needs to be briefly mentioned. Discovering how God can use you to introduce FIRST STEPS to others is very important. Share with old and new friends how God's power through Jesus Christ transformed your life.

Of course, make sure you're clean and living drug-free and addiction-free before you do so. Once you're on the road to recovery and renewal, invite others to make the journey with you.

> Once you're on the road to recovery,
> invite others to make the journey with you.

People who help others find they are helped and strengthened in the process. Instead of turning others onto bad things, you can help them find their way to the sunrise of a brand new day and a brand new life. Ask anyone who's come out of addiction what it's like to be useful instead of destructive, and they will tell you what great joy this gives them.

Step Twelve of AA says, "Having had a spiritual awakening as the result of these steps, we tried to carry this message to [other] alcoholics, and to practice these principles in all our affairs."

Each one of us has a valuable story to tell. We may be shy and feel awkward about speaking. We may think that what we have to share is too trivial. Is it actually going to help anyone else? We may struggle to get beyond the shame of our past experiences.

But our recovery story can help others who are trapped where we were. Are we willing to allow God to use us to help free others? Within each personal journey from bondage to freedom is a microcosm of the Gospel. When people hear our story, even if it seems trivial, we are offering them the chance to loosen their chains and begin their own journey.

(THE RECOVERY BIBLE)

In summary, your next steps involve two very important things; one is a private act and the other a public activity. I am referring to the reading and studying of God's Word and getting involved in a church. You can study the Bible as a part of the local church, if it offers such opportunities. Whether it does or doesn't, still it's imperative to begin a daily habit of reading the Bible on your own.

I recommend going to a Christian bookstore and buying what is called a One-Year Bible. It will have a reading for each day throughout the year, and by the end of one year you will have read through the entire Bible. That's a great accomplishment.

> Your next steps involve two very important things: Reading and studying God's Word and getting involved in a church.

When you take these "next steps," you will be on the way to follow in all the steps Christ has asked us to follow to serve Him, including serving others.

Many who fall back to old habits and lifestyles do so because they lack discipline; or to put it another way, they are spiritually lazy. The best defense against sin is having a good offense. In football, if the offense controls the ball, they eventually score; and they don't have to play defense as long as they are on the offensive. Having a daily practice of prayer and reading the Bible is to stay on the offense against temptation and sin. *"I have hidden your word in my heart, that I might not sin against you"* (Psalm 119:11).

"Let my supplication come before You; deliver me according to Your word" (Psalm 119:170, NKJV). This scripture sums up the two most important steps for believers: prayer and the entrance of the Word into our hearts, minds, and souls.

Chapter Eight

HOW TO AVOID A RELAPSE

"Now to Him who is able to keep you from stumbling, and to present you faultless before the presence of His glory with exceeding joy."

(JUDE 24, NKJV)

I'm sure you know those who tried to turn their lives around and maybe were clean for a while, but then fell back. Yes, relapse is always a possibility. It does not, however, need to be inevitable for you.

Some secular programs say that relapse is simply a part of recovery. That is not what faith-based programs believe, nor is this the normative experience for thousands who have taken the FIRST STEP and have been changed God's way.

Yes, there are temptations, very strong ones. Yes, there are the lusts of the flesh that have to be overcome, sometimes daily. Yes, the Bible says that once you cross the line over to God's side you become a target of Satan. The Bible describes him as one who prowls around, looking for victims to devour (1 Peter 5:8).

No, Satan does not have to get you!

No, relapse is not a part of recovery.

The Bible describes the work of Jesus Christ as transformation. Jesus buries the old you and makes you a new person. Billy Graham wrote the following:

> *When you come to Christ, the Holy Spirit takes up residence in your heart. Something new is added to your life supernaturally. You are transformed by the renewing of your mind. A new power, a new dimension, a new ability to love, a new joy, a new peace—the Holy Spirit comes in and lives the Christian life through you.*
>
> (THE RECOVERY BIBLE)

Here are several promises of God that back up my positive conviction about an addict making it, rather than falling and failing. You can, as they say, take these promises to the bank and cash them!

- *"Don't copy the behavior and customs of this world, but let God transform you into a new person by changing the way you think. Then you will learn to know God's will for you, which is good and pleasing and perfect"* (Romans 12:2).

- *"Our old sinful selves were crucified with Christ so that sin might lose its power in our lives. We are no longer slaves to sin. For when we died with Christ we were set free from the power of sin"* (Romans 6:6,7).

There is one word that the recovery movement uses that I agree with. That's the word "powerless." Step One of the Twelve Steps of Alcoholics Anonymous says: "We admitted we were powerless over alcohol—that our lives had become unmanageable."

The answer to this is to find Someone who can give us the ability to have power over our powerlessness. Jesus is the Higher Power of all higher powers. Paul the apostle said it's possible to throw off the old you and your former way of life, which he called *"rotten through and through, full of lust and sham"* (Ephesians 4:22, TLB).

> The answer is to find Someone who can give us power over our powerlessness. Jesus is the Higher Power of all higher powers.

What if you've taken the FIRST STEP of faith in God and have prayed that your life be changed, and things go well for a while, but then you stumble and fall?

My answer is this: There is a difference between a relapse and falling down.

Falling down is a one-time thing, or a temporary backsliding. A relapse, however, is going back to your old lifestyle. What you do after the first misstep is of great importance. You can immediately confess it to God (and to a trusted friend), or you can become so sorry for yourself that you stay down, and don't try to get up and walk again on God's path. It's much harder to recover after a relapse than a fall.

Everyone who has relapsed after walking for a time with the Lord and in freedom tells me that it's far worse going back to the life of addiction. This is due to the guilt and the deep sense of failure. Failure after having a time of being clean is worse than the initial failure of addiction. Some very famous people quit drugs: Elvis Presley quit. Jerry Garcia quit. Kurt Cobain quit, and so did Chris Farley and Anna Nicole Smith. It took death for them to quit. Let this be a warning: Quit God's way or death's way.

The Bible is very blunt about those who go back to the practices of the old life. Listen to these strong words from the Scriptures:

> *"And when people escape from the wickedness of the world by knowing our Lord and Savior Jesus Christ and then get tangled up and enslaved by sin again, they are worse*

off than before." Then it goes on and compares this to "a dog [that] returns to its vomit" and "a washed pig [that] returns to the mud"

(2 PETER 2:20,22).

Although having a fall or even a relapse is characteristic of some who have overcome life-controlling problems, it does not have to happen to you. If someone attends AA, it's almost expected that a person will relapse—and do so more than once. No studies have been done on the frequency of relapse. The fact is, many do not fall or return to their old habits and their old way of life. You can be one who does not fall.

> Many do not fall or return to their old habits. You can be one who does not fall.

Nevertheless, it is good to be prepared, lest the unfortunate should happen to you. Knowing why it happens can help prevent it. Let me list some reasons for relapses:

1. **Not having a 100 percent desire to stay clean, and not having the belief that a total cure is possible.**

If the addict has been exposed to the erroneous teaching that addiction/alcoholism is an *incurable disease* and that one has to learn to live with the disease, this can set the addict up for failure, for sure. Having a *disease mentality* means that you consciously or subconsciously expect to fall, for after all, if you think you have a permanent disease, it's going to manifest itself again.

This enables the addict to *shift the blame* from him or herself to the disease. The disease theory of addiction does irreparable damage to the mind of the addict. (And it is a theory, for there is no scientific evidence whatsoever of there being an addictive gene in the brain leading to addiction.) This can relieve a person of all responsibility for the addiction. If he relapses, he can say the disease caused it, it was not by the addict's personal choice. Augustine wrote, "Before God can deliver us, we must undeceive ourselves."

What is the disease model of addiction? Here's a quote from a secular, but reliable source:

> *At first, it seems hard to understand what is meant by saying that something a person regularly does [such as drinking alcohol] is a disease. Habitual, voluntary behavior of this sort does not resemble what we normally think of a disease, like cancer or diabetes. What is more, AA—and even hospital programs for alcoholism—doesn't actually treat biological causes of addiction. After all the claims are heard in the past decade about biological discoveries concerning alcoholism, not one of these findings has been translated into a usable treatment. Instead, the same group discussions that have been used for the last fifty years are*

employed in hospital programs...It is disturbing that an approach to addiction that is widely claimed to be scientific is actually false and is more harmful than beneficial."

(*THE TRUTH ABOUT ADDICTION AND RECOVERY: WHY ALCOHOLISM, DRUG ABUSE, SMOKING, OVEREATING, AND OTHER ADDICTIONS ARE NOT DISEASES,* BY STANTON PEELE, PH.D., AND ARCHIE BRODSKY)

If you think you are incurable, then you are: *"For as he thinks in his heart, so is he"* (Proverbs 23:7, NKJV). Someone has called the disease theory of addiction "stinking thinking." This is not the only reason why relapses occur, but it's a major one.

If you give yourself 100 percent to Christ, then He will give you a 100 percent cure. One former addict told me, "When I was on drugs, I was dedicated. You have to be to make it, and to get high. Sometimes I'd stand in the rain for hours waiting for my drug pusher to come so I could buy a bag of heroin. I was an addict 24/7. Now that I'm serving the Lord, I realize I need to give Him no less than what I gave the devil, and what I used to give to be a drug addict."

> If you give yourself 100 percent to Christ,
> He will give you a 100 percent cure.

Those who relapse do so for a variety of reasons, and one of them is because there is not a commitment that is sincere and total. You can't have one foot toward God and the other in the world. Jesus said no one who looks back is fit for His kingdom (Luke 9:62).

Neither can your motive be to get rid of your addiction so you can enjoy other sins. This I have seen way too often. There is a great danger when you empty the house of your heart of very bad things so you can partake of lesser bad things (things you may consider not that bad). A great preacher of the past, Charles Spurgeon, gives this warning:

> Suppose a house is attacked by seven thieves. The good man of the house has arms within, and he manages to kill six of the thieves. But if one survives, and he permits him to range his house, he may still be robbed, perhaps still slain...And if I have had seven evil vices, and by the grace of God six of those have been driven out, if I yet indulge and pamper the one that remains, I am still a lost man.

Victor Alfsen said, "God can do wonders with a broken heart if you give him all the pieces."

It's got to be serious business when we are giving ourselves to God and to His Son, Jesus Christ. This is not like stepping into a swimming pool or ocean water on a beach for recreation. This is about *re-creation*. The step I'm talking about is a step toward life and away from death. It's nothing to trifle with. If the approach to God is, "Well, let me try it and see if it works," this is treating God like He's some kind of experimental medicine.

In the Bible, during the early history of the children of Israel in the Old Testament, they had been set free from years of captivity in Egypt. God performed many miracles for them as He led them to a new land that was to be their very own place of lasting freedom from slavery. They had many missteps along the way from Egypt to the Promised Land. At one point, their leader, Joshua, called upon the people to do what everyone must do when following the Lord God. Here's how Joshua presented the challenge to them: *"Choose today whom you will serve"* (Joshua 24:15). It was all or nothing, or as someone has put it, "Either Jesus is Lord of all or He is not Lord at all."

I am often asked how many people are cured who go through Teen Challenge's one-year, faith-based residential rehabilitation program. My answer is that there are no failures in God—there is a 100 percent cure when a person gives himself 100 percent to God's way.

> There are no failures in God—there is a 100 percent cure when a person gives himself 100 percent to God's way.

Martin Luther said, "I have held many things in my hands, and I have lost them all; but whatever I have placed in God's hands, that I still possess."

When our FIRST STEP to God is a sincere, firm, and purposeful step (not half-hearted, wishful thinking), it will be a step into a life of no-turning-back and no missteps.

The door to salvation in Jesus Christ is not a revolving door; it's a door that has no handle on the other side from which one seeks to escape when the going gets tough.

2. **Make sure you understand that true repentance before God, mixed with faith, is a part of your prayer for deliverance from a life-controlling problem.**

Relapse may occur when there has been no repentance before God. God does not put addicts in one category and everyone else in another. Being addicted to gambling, sex, drugs, or alcohol is not a worse sin than others. However, these are sins that take place, not just before family or society, but also before God.

It is God who is offended by sinful behavior. We are sinners before God before we're sinners before society or our family. We have to deal with God first, and get our record with Him cleared up. Only Jesus can do this.

Repentance is being sorry before God—not sorry for having been caught, or sorry about the trouble addiction causes, but sorry for transgressing against a holy God and shutting Him out of our lives. FIRST STEP requires a godly sorrow for having disobeyed Christ's call to follow Him. Anyone would be sorry for ending up in court to face charges for breaking man's law. The true type of sorrow needed, the one that leads to repentance, is sorrow over breaking God's law.

False sorrow is when you just regret all the bad things that happen to you while carrying out an addictive lifestyle. Who isn't sorry about going to prison, getting sick, having an overdose, being broke, getting drunk and making a fool of oneself, getting beat up, losing a job or any number of adverse things that happen when hanging around dangerous places, dangerous people, and participating in risky behavior. This is sorrow that should lead one to try to change, but it usually doesn't.

This is why it takes a power greater than the power of drugs, booze, sex, and loose living to get free. This is why a FIRST STEP toward God is so important.

Repentance is like the cry of a newborn baby, which indicates the child is alive. That cry is, or should be, this: *"O God, be merciful to me, for I am a sinner"* (Luke 18:13).

The Bible differentiates between the sorrow that is temporary and has nothing to do with how we feel about our relationship to God, and godly sorrow that is evidence of true repentance. *"The kind of sorrow God wants us to experience leads us away from sin and results in salvation."* The same verse just quoted goes on to say, *"There's no regret for that kind of sorrow. But worldly sorrow, which lacks repentance, results in spiritual death"* (2 Corinthians 7:10). Repentance is disgust for the life we lived without God. This disgust is so strong that we want to turn away from sin, totally and completely, and never go back.

> Repentance is disgust for the life
> we lived without God, a disgust so strong
> that we want to turn away from sin
> and never go back.

A mother taught her young son about repentance with the following poem:

Repentance is to leave
the sin we loved before;
and show that we in earnest grieve
by doing so no more.

This mother might have gotten this from Martin Luther, for it was he who said, "To do so no more is the truest repentance."

One of the most fundamental marks of true repentance is a disposition to see our sins as God sees them. I see too many who are sorry for themselves, and not sorry before God. Our sin made it necessary for God to give us His *"one and only Son, so that everyone who believes in him will not perish but have eternal life"* (John 3:16).

If you can look on sin without sorrow, then you have never looked on Christ. A faith look at Jesus breaks the heart both for sin and from sin.

(CHARLES SPURGEON)

Beware of excusing your dependency based on a self-deception that you have no control over it. You must take responsibility for your problems. No one forces you to do what you do. If you have reaped a bad harvest from your actions, it's because you have sown the seeds of bad choices that you have made. The Bible says, *"You will always harvest what you plant! Those who live only to satisfy their own sinful nature will harvest decay and death from that sinful nature. But those who live to please the Spirit will harvest everlasting life from the Spirit"* (Galatians 6:7,8).

The law of sowing and reaping can also work to our benefit. The prophet Hosea wrote, *"Plant the good seeds of righteousness, and you will harvest a crop of love. Plow up the hard ground of your hearts, for now is the time to seek the LORD, that he may come and shower righteousness upon you"* (Hosea 10:12).

How can you plow up the hard ground of your heart? Give God an account through confession of all the trash you have accumulated (this is repentance), and God will take out the garbage! Give it all to Him. Showers of blessing will follow.

> Give God an account through confession of all the trash you have accumulated, and He will take out the garbage!

3. **Make sure you make new connections in the faith community as seriously as you made connections in your old life.**

Anyone who leaves behind old habits also must leave behind old friends and the old crowd. *New connections* in the church world, as written about in the previous chapter, are vital not only because it's the place where spiritual life is found, but it's also a refuge away from the old stomping grounds. Anyone who does not break away from the places and people of the past will never be free from old habits and addictions. The old friends and the crowds are sometimes a part of the package of destructive behavior.

The Bible says, *"Therefore, come out from among unbelievers, and separate yourselves from them, says the LORD. Don't touch their filthy things, and I will welcome you"* (2 Corinthians 6:17). A few verses previous to this, the question is asked, *"What harmony can there be between Christ and the devil?"* (2 Corinthians 6:15).

There is an environment, an atmosphere in which a person engages in drugs and other so-called pleasures. In my dealings with drug addicts, alcoholics, gangs, and even prostitutes, they often are as much addicted to the places where they engage in such activities as to the practice itself. One must be set free from the people and places of vices as well as the vices themselves.

When [Christ] asks you to do something, it is only to help you get free. For instance, you will have to get rid of your old friends who dragged you down. Jesus said, *"If anyone is a friend of the world, he is an enemy to me."* He also said, *"No man can serve two masters."* Why does Christ demand this of you? Only because He knows they will tear down everything He builds up in you. They will infect you with their wicked viruses. You are asked [to do this], not for His sake, but for yours.

(DAVID WILKERSON)

Connection to Christ requires disconnection from the world. Changed people change their lifestyle. They go and hang out in the faith community. They find new friends. They get involved in church and Christian activities.

> Connection to Christ requires disconnection from the world. Changed people change their lifestyle. They go and hang out in the faith community.

This also means getting involved in the mission of the church; that is, taking the message of freedom from life-controlling problems to others. This is one of *the most important* discoveries someone makes in creating new connections in the church. They find a new purpose in life. This includes being a role model and a messenger to those still in the old life on how they can take the FIRST STEP toward a new beginning and a new life.

Your mission gives your life meaning. William James said, "The best use of life is to spend it for something that outlasts you." The truth is, only the kingdom of God is going to last. *Everything* else will vanish. That is why we must live purpose-driven lives—lives committed to worship, fellowship, spiritual growth, ministry, and fulfilling our mission on earth. The results of these activities *will* last—forever!

> We must live purpose-driven lives committed to worship, fellowship, spiritual growth, ministry, and fulfilling our mission on earth.

Rick Warren writes in *The Purpose Driven Life*:

There are people on the planet that only you can reach, because of where you live and what God has made you to be. If just one person will be in heaven because of you, your life will have made a difference for eternity. Start looking around at your personal mission field and pray, "God, who have you put in my life for me to tell about Jesus?"

Sometimes it can be hard to find and build new relationships with the faith community in the church.

Don't expect to be welcomed in the church like a long-lost prodigal, unless you once were a part of the church to which you return after accepting Christ or renewing your commitment to Christ after having backslid. In fact, if you return to a church where family and friends have known your failed past, they may be slow to accept and forgive you. Hopefully not, but you need to be prepared if you are not given a hero's welcome.

If you graduated from a one-year, faith-based rehab program, you may be accustomed to having attended various churches where you gave your testimony. You may have been received with admiration and applause for this. It may not happen in your "home" church, or a church you hope to call home. People may rejoice at your conversion when they are not close to you, but then treat you different when you fellowship with them on a regular basis. Again, hopefully this is not the case, but it could be. You need to be serious about making new connections, even in the face of resistance. There are believers who will open their hearts, church, and even home to you. Find them! There are multitudes of them. If you are persistent in your walk with God and in your desire to identify with the "Body of Christ" (the church), you will find them.

Someone has said that "Satan watches for those vessels [ships] that sail without a convoy [travel without being accompanied by other ships]." We are more open to temptation when we forsake the assembling of ourselves together with the people of God (Hebrews 10:25).

The great apostle Paul once was a religious terrorist and arrested Christians. Then one day he had a miraculous conversion on the road to Damascus, where he was about to carry out another attack on the new Jesus believers. After some time, he then went to meet with the very same believers he was attacking, and naturally they were suspicious. *"When Saul [Paul] arrived in Jerusalem [to present himself as one of them], he tried to meet with the believers, but they were all afraid of him. They did not believe he had truly become a believer!"* (Acts 9:26). It took the intervention and testimony of another well-respected member of the Christian church community, Barnabas, to verify his conversion before he was accepted.

Whatever it takes, make fresh and new contacts in the faith community. It's the only organization that exists primarily for those who are not members. They are the new family to which God has called you to belong. Rick Warren writes:

> *Your spiritual family is even more important than your physical family, because it will last forever. Our families on earth are wonderful gifts from God, but they are temporary and fragile, often broken by divorce, distance, growing old, and inevitably death. On the other hand, our spiritual family—our relationship to other believers—will*

continue throughout eternity. It is a much stronger union,
a more permanent bond, than blood relationships.

As John Wesley said, "The Bible knows nothing of solitary religion."

4. **If relapse occurs, humble yourself and ask Christ to forgive you, restore you, and return you to the place where you were spiritually before you fell.**

Maybe you did not submit your all to Christ in the first place. You need to repeat the FIRST STEP and this time, surrender your entire life to Christ.

The hardest thing a person has to deal with after having been on top of the mountain, spiritually speaking, is the embarrassment of the fall. They often avoid the very people and places where their help came from originally.

They also often go deeper into addiction to avoid the guilt from the fall or relapse.

If you are in relapse right now or trying to come back from a fall, humble yourself before God and others and come back into the Light. You are not the first person to backslide. In the Bible, King David committed adultery and arranged for the woman's husband to be purposely placed in the front of the battlefield so he would be killed. Peter, a disciple of Jesus, blatantly denied he was a follower of Christ during Jesus' trial. The children of Israel, God's chosen people, turned to idol worship over and over again.

In all the cases mentioned above, and many more, God was always ready to forgive when the backslider asked for forgiveness. For example, King David said, *"I recognize my rebellion; it haunts me day and night. Against you, and you alone, have I sinned; I have done what is evil in your sight."* This was part of David's prayer in Psalm 51. It can and should be your prayer as well.

Did David give up? Did he run and hide from God and the people he let down? No. He called out to the Lord. The rest of David's prayer of confession and restoration continues in Psalm 51:

> *You desire honesty...Purify me from my sins, and I will be clean; wash me, and I will be whiter than snow. Oh, give me back my joy again...Create in me a clean heart, O God. Renew a loyal spirit within me...Restore to me the joy of your salvation, and make me willing to obey you.*
>
> (PSALM 51:3–12)

God did just what David asked. He will do the same for you.

Part Three

FIRST STEPS FOR INTERVENERS

Chapter Nine

STEPS TOWARD INTERVENTION

What are the first crucial steps that families and loved ones of someone with a life-controlling problem can take to help them? Knowing what to do first and also *what not to do* is of utmost importance.

Here is some helpful advice.

1. Before taking any steps, analyze the problem adequately and realistically.

Overreacting can be just as harmful as underreacting. For example, a teenager who is caught smoking marijuana for the first time is not necessarily an addict. There is a difference between a young man curiously surfing the net, running across X-rated photographs, and someone who does it habitually. College students involved in binge drinking hopefully will mature and not become captive to the beer can or bottle. Be sure that the label *addict* or *alcoholic* accurately applies to the individual you're trying to help. I don't mean to imply that a person who is in a pre-addiction phase should not be helped, but labeling someone an addict who is not can drive the person away from you. The distinction between drug user and drug addict may be unclear to those trying to help someone, but to the user this distinction is important.

True assessment is important as an initial step to determining whether a person is out of control or in the early stages of abuse, which may lead to a potential problem. However, the purpose of this chapter is what to do when a person is in whatever stage of drug and/or alcohol use (or the other harmful practices being discussed here). Unfortunately, many families do not realize there is a problem until it reaches the addictive stage.

> True assessment is important as an initial step to determining whether a person is out of control or in the early stages of abuse, which may lead to a potential problem.

What do you do with those who lie, run, con, and are in total denial that they have a problem?

2. The first step in this case is to *confront with compassion.*

Confrontation and compassion seem to be opposite reactions. Anger never helps. It is possible to be firm with someone needing help without being angry. The Bible tells us to *"speak the truth in love"* (Ephesians 4:15), and the modern term of this is called "tough love."

What should make confrontation easier for believers is having the assurance that they are not alone. When families and loved ones bring the situation to the Lord in prayer, they can be assured that the Holy Spirit has gone before them to prepare the heart of the person needing help to receive it. This does not mean intervention is not met with resistance. Praying family members having to confront someone are strengthened through prayer to not give in or give up when they are met with denial or resistance.

What reaction can you expect when confronting those who need to make a drastic change in their behavior? Alcoholics deny. Drug addicts run and avoid the issue. Those addicted to Internet porn usually will not admit they have a problem unless caught red-handed. Gamblers may downplay the seriousness of the problem until the family finances are drastically affected.

Other responses to expect are:

- Childlike temper tantrums
- Table turning:
  - "What I'm doing is no worse than what you do."
  - "You're so judgmental."
  - "You've betrayed me by telling others about this."
  - "It's none of their business."
- Silence and avoidance
- Defense mechanisms
- Rationalizing:
  - "You don't understand the pressure I'm under at my job."
- Minimizing:
  - "It's my business. I'm not hurting anyone else, only myself."

When individuals reach that stage of alcoholism or addiction, they will rarely submit to a family member's call for them to take measures to help themselves without strong and firm confrontation. Threats, coercion, or bullying tactics rarely work. Neither will passivity! The addict will do everything possible to deny, delay, or do anything to keep from asking for help. Studies have shown that those pressured and coerced into getting treatment have less success than those who go willingly.

Sometimes it takes a team of people to do the confronting. Betty Ford, the wife of the late President Gerald Ford, became a model to many people when she finally admitted she was an alcoholic. However, she did so only when her entire family confronted her and would not back down until she went for help. One thing is for sure: Parents and other family members need to be united in their efforts to get a substance abuser to seek help. If one parent is for confrontation and the other is not, you can be sure the abuser will exploit this to the fullest.

The confronting team should be made up of someone the person knows, but who is not emotionally involved with the abuser's problems and addictive behavior. It may be a younger or older sibling, or someone the person may have grown up with and has good memories of doing things with before the addictive behavior started. If such individuals are perceived as knowledgeable, concerned for the addict's welfare, and somehow impartial, their recommendation can go a long way toward motivating the person to get treatment.

> The confronting team should be made up of someone the person knows, but who is not emotionally involved with the other person's problems and addictive behavior.

Look for people who have possible *influence* and *leverage* with this person. When I speak of leverage, I mean that if the help is resisted, the confrontational team would be able to consider taking steps that may compel the addict to change his mind. I encourage parents, for example, to not bail out a teenager who is in trouble with the law until they are confronting the issue, using the possibility of jail time as leverage.

> *Without sufficient leverage, even the best-organized confrontation sometimes fails. To determine whether or not you possess leverage, ask yourself: What do I have (or do) which the alcoholic/addict depends on that might be hard for him or her to replace?*
>
> (*FREEING SOMEONE YOU LOVE FROM ALCOHOL AND DRUGS,*
> BY RONALD L. ROGERS AND CHANDLER SCOTT MCMILLAN)

A spouse who has the option of living temporarily with family or friends can threaten to leave until the other gets help.

To use leverage properly, the intervention team must be prepared to offer a choice: "Either you go for help, or we take something away from you." This might include taking away financial support, friendship, or even the place of residence. (Of course, if this is not carried out, the situation will probably get worse.)

"Either go for treatment [or seek help such as a FIRST STEP], or continue as you have been. Only this time without our participation, support, and help."

Given such dramatic choices, most addicts will cooperate with the plan presented to them. This is because the "plan" is easier to accept than to refuse and be further alienated from the team of helpers.

People who should not be involved in intervention are those who react rather than act and cannot keep their emotions in check, such as those who freeze up in tense situations or who feel that confrontation is wrong. When we confront rebellious students in our program, I often send two people into the counseling session: one with the gift of mercy and the other with the gift of discernment! While one speaks softly, the other lays down the law. This is what might be called the "good cop, bad cop" concept.

3. Confrontation needs to be preceded by a lot of prayer.

Sometimes family members are so stressed out and so tired of the games addicts play, they find it hard to pray. In this case, enlist the prayers of others.

It is not necessary to publicize that you have an addict in the family, but neither is it good to hide this fact at all costs. Share it with a few select friends who know how to pray. If you gather a team of compassionate confronters to face your spouse, parent, child, sibling, or whoever, it's ideal to have special prayer going on at the time of the meeting. (The next chapter is on developing a prayer team.)

Be sure that you go into such a meeting with a rescue plan. If the person is not ready for a FIRST STEP approach for help, then it's important to make contact with whatever appropriate program is best for this person at the time. When the problem is more psychological, a referral to a Christian therapist may be what is initially needed.

Is it appropriate for a Christian family to refer someone to a non-Christian program? The addict or alcoholic may have a negative bias toward a Christian program due to some past experiences in a church or with Christians. This should be taken into account if the person is willing to go for help, but does not want a faith-based or Christ-centered program. A FIRST STEP toward recovery may be to go to a secular program, and hopefully later to a faith-based one.

A person who is physically addicted to a chemical substance may need to go to a detox center.

Sometimes a person needing help can only take a baby step before taking an adult step. Reading this book may be the FIRST STEP toward the big FIRST STEP to God.

> Sometimes a person needing help
> can only take a baby step before
> taking an adult step.

When confronting with compassion, the person may at first mistake compassion for weakness. This requires a firm, loving, and caring response that lets the person know you will not back off. The mistake parents and families often make is to give the addict "one more chance." This is not compassion, but rather enabling the person to get over one more time on the family. "Getting over" is another way of saying the user has conned the family.

The reason so many addicts "get over" or con their parents and spouses is because families engage in behavior called "enabling." This is when the family makes excuses, covers up, and tries to rescue the addict from the consequences of his own irresponsible behavior.

When the family and loved ones make a decision to stop enabling, they may see things initially go from bad to worse. This is a critical time for parents especially. A mother's reaction may be, "I can't stand to see my child in such pain and danger," or "My child might get killed, and I can't let that happen." However, this is a time to stand fast. Enablers prolong addictions. Once a decision is made to no longer protect this person, in the short run things may get worse. Experience shows that only consequences bring addicts to the reality of their problem.

> Experience shows that only consequences bring addicts to the reality of their problem.

During the dark times of witnessing an addict's downward spiral, the Christian family must trust God. You can rest assured that God knows where your child is, no matter how deep the sin. His love surpasses even your love. So stop enabling! Stop feeding the problem, and stop deceiving yourself and trust in Him instead. Jesus promises to give us wisdom to make the difficult decisions, and He stands ready and waiting with open arms to help those who really want help.

What about ultimatums? "If you don't go for help, I'm going to tell your boss," or "I'm going to contact the school authorities," or "You're going to have to find another place to live." Reserve this one as a last resort.

Parents often ask, "What should I do with my teenager who is out of control using drugs?"

My advice is to lay down rules and if not obeyed to find an alternative living arrangement for them, especially if younger siblings are in the home. One couple told their son that if his drug use continued he would have to sleep in the garage until he was of legal age, at which time he would then be escorted off the property. Putting them out is a last resort, but usually they have friends where they can stay. Addicts are great survivors living in a drug culture. I know many adolescents who when told to leave home then asked for help. However, there are no easy answers to this question, and every family deals with this in different ways.

Parents have a right to set boundaries and retain their dignity and standards.

In the process of trying to free someone you love from addictive activities, there are FIRST STEPS that the helpers need to take for themselves. Too often, those who are the victims of a loved one's life-controlling problem fail to realize the effect it's having on them. Families also deny themselves the right to the help they need because they're so caught up in trying to save someone, not realizing they're drowning in the process.

4. The first step for the interveners is allowing God to take care of you.

Most parents, spouses, and family members involved in a long-term effort to save another family member get very drained, spiritually and emotionally. Often when the addicted individual is ready for help, the helper is not in the best condition to be there for that person. When the family is needed the most, it's quite possible that all their energies have already been spent in helping the addict or alcoholic to finally make that decision to get help.

> One of the first things we tell our clients is: "You need to put yourself back at the top of your priority list." There is no way to help someone else until you first take care of your needs, your pain, and yourself.
>
> (*CONCERNED INTERVENTION* BY JOHN & PAT O'NEILL)

Staying close to God through His Word and in prayer helps keep hope alive! In my own family a brother became an alcoholic, yet we (especially my mother) never gave up. We waited decades for the answer to come—and it did. He has now been free from his addiction for decades.

It is good to have a prayer partner, someone with whom you can have times of prayer together as well as share your feelings in times of discouragement. One of the feelings most often dealt with by parents is guilt. What did I/we do to contribute to our child's addiction? Don't feel ashamed about feeling guilty; this is normal. Most parents and families experience this. Part of the FIRST STEPS for interveners is to stop blaming yourself. It has always caught my attention when two or three children are raised in a dysfunctional family, and yet only one goes astray. Why is this? Because we all make our choices and our choices turn around and make us, for better or worse.

The problem of guilt and responsibility is addressed in the Old Testament. Ezekiel 18:1,2 says, *"Why do you quote this proverb concerning the land of Israel: 'The parents have eaten sour grapes, but their children's mouths pucker at the taste'?"* Apparently some Israelites tried to blame their parents for their evil conduct. The Lord said neither the parents were guilty before God for their child's sin, nor the child for the parents' wrongdoing. *"The person who sins is the one who will die. The child will not be punished for the parent's sins, and the parent will not be punished for the child's sins. Righteous people will be rewarded for their own righteous behavior, and wicked people will be punished for their own wickedness...Therefore, I will judge each of you, O people of Israel, according to your actions, says the Sovereign LORD. Repent, and turn from your sins. Don't let them destroy you!"* (Ezekiel 18:20,30).

The message today to parents is, "Don't let your children's sins and problems put you under condemnation. Each of us will be judged before a sovereign and merciful God."

> Don't let your children's sins and problems put you under condemnation.

This does not mean if parents did do wrong by their children, they don't suffer. The scars of our sins often remain long after they are forgiven and forsaken. However, parents need to separate their responsibility from their children's. Parents need to confess before God things they may have done that affected their children. Yet, at the same time, understand that God holds the children responsible for the choices they make. If we keep looking at the past, we will not have the strength to deal with the present and the future.

Also, you'd be surprised how forgiving most children are of their parents. In time, they will remember the good times experienced together more than the bad.

Judi Braddy, author of *Prodigal in the Parsonage*, writes from the experience of seeing her adolescent son spiral into a crisis of destructive behavior that lasted twenty years. She writes:

Judging from the correspondence when my book was published, it's common for parents to experience myriad emotions when their children go astray—disbelief, sadness, humiliation, anger, guilt and depression just to name a few.

From the *Pentecostal Evangel*, Feb. 25, 2007, article entitled "A Comforter for Concerned Moms":

Too often we carry all the blame for their bad behavior, to the point we become consumed by our feelings of failure. This can hinder us from seeking a spiritual solution. As long as the enemy keeps us focusing inward, we forget to look upward...I finally came to realize the choices my son was making had little to do with us. We were merely the closest, most convenient symbol of authority against which to vent his anger. Like Eden's first pair of prodigals, his rebellion was against God.

There are times when it is necessary for parents to ask a teenager or adult son or daughter to forgive them. Some parents do to their children what their parents did to them.

This is not to excuse bad parenting, but it is an effort to try to get children to understand why parents sometimes do regretful things in raising them.

One more important word to parents, spouses, and other family members dealing with a sheep gone astray: Don't neglect the "good" kids in the family. Parents who have a child with a severe physical or mental disorder of necessity spend so much time handling the sick child's problem that they unconsciously can neglect the other healthy children. The same can be said for families dealing with one member's addiction. The kids doing well can suffer in silence or, God forbid, do something wrong to get attention.

> Don't neglect the "good" kids in the family. The kids doing well can suffer in silence or, God forbid, do something wrong to get attention.

Before, during, and following intervention, families of addicts should saturate themselves with the Word of God, trusting in God's promises (especially those that deal with the salvation and deliverance of children and loved ones.) For example, here are three promises from God that parents, spouses, grandparents, and family members can claim as they are approaching a time of intervention with their addicted loved one, or when intervention efforts have not succeeded.

- *"This promise is to you, to your children, and to those far away—all who have been called by the Lord our God"* (Acts 2:39). The "promise" in this verse refers to the previous verse, which says that "in the name of Jesus Christ" there is the forgiveness of sin. This promise is for all children today who are "far away" from God. We need to believe that our wayward, rebellious and prodigal children will hear God's call for them to come to Him.

- *"Your children will be like vigorous young olive trees as they sit around your table"* (Psalm 128:3). The entire chapter of Psalm 128 is encouraging, as it is a promise to those who fear the Lord and follow in His ways. It says, *"You will enjoy the fruit of your labor"* (v. 2). The fruit of our labor, I believe, refers to the efforts, the labors of having raised our children as well as the "labor" in prayer on behalf of their return and redemption. The picture of our children sitting at our table in health may not be true now, but it can become reality to those who keep the faith.

- Here is a wonderful promise for parents of disobedient children, whatever age they might be: *"'Look around you and see, for all your children will come back to you. As surely as I live,' says the LORD, 'they will be like jewels or bridal ornaments for you to display'"* (Isaiah 49:18). This is also a promise to claim for a wife whose husband is an addict, or vice versa.

Chapter Ten

FROM DENIAL TO DECISION

Getting a person who needs help to take the FIRST STEP, any step, is an incredible challenge. It takes years before some addicts are ready. Unfortunately, some never take the step into freedom, but instead take a step into prison or worse, death. Many a family has exhausted every possible effort they know of (along with their finances) in trying to get a loved one to find the path to a new life.

There are several ways you, or your loved one, can begin to find total healing from addiction, such as:

- Enter a private rehabilitation program.
- Enroll in a faith-based residential program like Teen Challenge. (They accept adults, and not just teens.)

- Find a Twelve-Step Program such as Alcoholics Anonymous (AA) or Narcotics Anonymous, Gambler Anonymous, or similar groups. The latter two groups are patterned after the Twelve-Step Program of Alcoholics Anonymous.
- Find a Twelve-Step small group, a Christian program provided by a local church (if possible) such as Celebrate Recovery, or Living Free.
- Find a friend or a group of friends committed to helping the addict to get clean by having the person make a commitment to quit, and becoming accountable to the group to stay clean.

What if you (or your loved one) are not ready to receive the help you need? It's important to understand some of the obstacles that may yet be in the way. There are usually three reasons why an addict or alcoholic does not seek help.

1. Denial

"I am not an alcoholic," or, "I am not addicted to drugs. Yes, I may use drugs, but I'm certainly not an addict!" The same denials are used by those involved in what I call the lesser-known addictions. Without a doubt, denial is the number one way to simply avoid facing the need for help. Denial is a protective device, a defense to protect oneself from painful truths and realities. Both users and their families can be in a state of denial. Denial is delay, and delay is what neither the addict nor the family can afford to do.

The other side of denial is when family and loved ones "see no evil" and are blind to what is going on right under their roof or nose. Christians are prone to denial because they are supposed to be people of faith and see the best in everyone. Parents, who love their children often sincerely, but naively, find it hard to exercise discernment and tough love.

> Christians are prone to denial because they are supposed to be people of faith and see the best in everyone.

The loved ones need to realize that from the perspective of addicts or alcoholics, the drug or drink is actually the addict's solution, and not the problem. It is what enables addicts to escape from painful realities surrounding them. Their denial is their shield from a life gone wrong.

2. Shame

Addicted people acknowledge to themselves and perhaps to others that they have a serious problem, but are either ashamed or too proud to take the responsibility to seek help. It's humbling both to admit your faults to those who love you, and then to possibly place yourself in the hands of strangers in some type of program if the choice is to do so.

Pride is a twin to shame. And denial and shame build walls that are almost impregnable. *"Haughtiness goes before destruction; humility precedes honor"* (Proverbs 18:12).

Shame leads to further drug or alcohol abuse to numb the pain of feeling like a failure. This becomes a vicious cycle. Drug abuse leads to shame—shame leads to more abuse.

It is through humility and brokenness that an addict is able to open up and listen to the voices of those who are seeking to help. AA has called this "bottoming out." Or, as someone has said, "It's on our backs that we're forced to look up." Loved ones need to "watch and pray" so that if the door of opportunity opens, even only a crack, it's time to introduce the addict to the steps God has ordained to begin walking toward the light.

> It is through humility and brokenness that an addict is able to open up and listen to the voices of those who are seeking to help.

3. Fear

There is the fear of the unknown of whatever program is being recommended to them—fear of being without the substances that, to abusers and addicts, have become their solution, not the problem. Most addicts will not seek help until the pain of addiction is greater than the pleasure they have derived from it.

> Most addicts will not seek help until the pain of addiction is greater than the pleasure they have derived from it.

Fear can be a good thing when the addict wakes up to realize that continued use and abuse is worse than seeking help.

How can these barriers to recovery, rehabilitation, and ultimate healing be overcome? How can the parent(s), spouse, or other interested helpers motivate the substance abuser to commit to a program or person that can help?

My experience in the field of addiction for the past five decades has been in helping young people overcome drug and alcohol addiction. Most of them want help. They are motivated either by wanting to overcome the pain of addiction, or wanting to come clean to relieve their loved ones of the suffering they are causing from their addiction.

> Most people want to overcome the pain of addiction, or want to come clean to relieve their loved ones of the suffering they are causing from their addiction.

Yet, countless parents and others appeal to me, asking, "How can I get my child (or spouse) to go into a program?"

If the addict is not willing, often nothing can be done.

Jesus spoke of those who refused to change and take any step toward Him. He said, *"God's light came into the world, but people loved the darkness more than the light, for their actions were evil. All who do evil hate the light and refuse to go near it for fear their sins will be exposed"* (John 3:19,20).

The fact is, some people have to get worse before they will seek to get better. There are others who under no circumstances will volunteer for any type of program or therapy that might help them. The darkness becomes their friend—their security. The good news is that such persons are the exception, not the rule. Most addicts eventually burn out and are forced by the circumstances surrounding their addiction to seek help. The darkness eventually becomes so agonizing that they are forced to humble themselves to family or friends and accept the help they need.

If family members can hold out long enough during the period of an addict's downward path and still be there when the person cries for help, there is hope. Proverbs 13:12 says, *"Hope deferred makes the heart sick."* This is God's way of saying it is normal to be heartsick over a loved one's life-controlling problem, especially when the person seems rebellious against all efforts to help. Hundreds of parents and spouses can testify, however, to the importance of working

FROM DENIAL TO DECISION

through the sense of hopelessness. One addict told me that every night when he came home high his mother pleaded with him to stop. He paid no attention to her until one night when she said nothing. He went to his room and cried, saying to himself, "My mother must not love me anymore. She quit hollering at me."

I know of mothers who refused to give up on their sons and daughters, even when their spouse gave up. Such mothers did what the Bible says in 1 Peter 1:13: *"Hope to the end"* (KJV).

When we don't know what else to do, we can still pray. Prayer connects us to Almighty God, and prayer teams can help bring about victory when all else fails.

Chapter Eleven

DEVELOPING A FIRST STEP PRAYER TEAM

"If you see a fellow believer sinning in a way that does not lead to death, you should pray, and God will give that person life."

(1 JOHN 5:16)

What I am sharing in this last chapter is for the parents and family of addicts, as well as for those who work with addicts, either informally or in an organized ministry within a church or faith-based rehab program.

For those who are serious in realizing that the FIRST STEP to a cure from addiction is to take prayer seriously, then this is for you. One of the greatest testimonies to the reality of Christianity is when we intercede before our Father God for those weakest and most wounded among us, especially those in our immediate family. *"But those who won't care for their own relatives, especially those in their own household, have denied the true faith. Such people are worse than unbelievers"* (1 Timothy 5:8).

During my years of working with hardcore addicts, I have seen what can happen when those ministering to the addict exercise spiritual authority through intercessory prayer with and for that person. What hours of counseling often cannot produce, prayer in a Spirit-filled atmosphere (in a church service or in a small-group prayer gathering) can. It can result in a miraculous deliverance for someone unable to overcome a life-controlling problem any other way.

> What hours of counseling often cannot produce, prayer in a Spirit-filled atmosphere can. It can result in a miraculous deliverance for someone unable to overcome a life-controlling problem any other way.

If you are not experienced in what I call "deliverance praying," it is possible to find churches that practice this kind of spiritual warfare. Find a church that does. I am referring to a group of Spirit-filled believers who lay hands on a person needing help, praying for a supernatural manifestation of God's power to come upon this person. This is scriptural, as the Bible says in James 5:14,15, *"Are any of you sick? You should call for the elders of the church to come and pray over you, anointing you with oil in the name of the Lord. [15] Such a prayer offered in faith will heal the sick, and the Lord will make you well. And if you have committed any sins, you will be forgiven."*

Some churches have trained and selected prayer warriors who pray over those physically or emotionally sick, especially during times of an "altar call" following the sermon. Other churches may do it more formally by having a prayer line in which the leaders of the church (often called elders) pray for a person needing physical, emotional, or psychological healing. In faith-based rehabilitation programs like Teen Challenge, residents are given opportunity during weekly chapel meetings to voluntarily respond to altar calls. The leaders and staff then pray for these individuals.

In working with hardcore addicts, I have participated in the laying on of hands with willing candidates, and have seen miraculous results. When counseling or Bible classes (as important as these two things are) did not change these addicts, a supernatural encounter with the presence of the living God through prayer has made the difference.

The same thing happens in churches when God's people are committed to intense, fervent prayer for those in bondage. The line of a gospel hymn goes like this: "At the cross where I first saw the light and the burden of my heart rolled away, it was there by faith I received my sight..." It is a shame that in many churches there are drug users, addicts, and pre-addicts of all types sitting in the congregation listening to a gospel message about the cross that talks about captives being set free. Yet, they are not invited to "see the light" or given an opportunity to be prayed for or to pray themselves and take that FIRST STEP to their freedom. A friend once said, "The church that does not practice what it preaches should be sued for malpractice!" Perhaps this is an extreme statement, yet the churches my friend had previously attended never encouraged him to take the all-important step to God in prayer.

One church that makes prayer a priority did some concentrated intercessory prayer to combat the flow of drugs into their region. The pastor and a friend drove to a place overlooking their city before sunrise and fervently prayed. Within a week, newspapers in local counties reported drug busts almost daily. "We knew we had hit the mark, the pastor acknowledged" The church also joined other churches for a concert of prayer to ask God to reduce the deaths of young people in their county to half of what they were for the same period the previous year.

If those who want to take the FIRST STEP prayer can find a church or a program that reaches out to addicts through fervent and passionate prayer, that person will be changed. I have no doubt about that. It's almost a cliché, but it's true that "prayer changes things." It is a shame that those who believe in prayer, theoretically, do it too passively and as an afterthought, rather than as a FIRST STEP. I do not mean to so emphasize prayer as a FIRST STEP so as to give the impression that this is some magical formula to a cure; but history and experience show that there is power, tremendous power, in prayer.

> Prayer is not some magical formula to a cure; but history and experience show that there is power, tremendous power, in prayer.

A word of caution: Beware of Christians who believe every problem, especially addiction, is a demon to be cast out. There are such cases of individuals with a serious life-controlling problem who are possessed by a demonic spirit. But my experience is that it's the exception, and not the rule.

If demonic spirits manifest themselves, find an experienced prayer warrior (particularly a pastor who has had experience in casting out demons) and seek his or her assistance. I do subscribe to what an old-time Pentecostal preacher told me years ago: "Some things have to be cast out; most things have to be *worked out*."

> Some things have to be *cast out*;
> most things have to be *worked out*.

It is not necessary to have someone on a prayer team with experience in casting out demons, but it is important to have those who know how to pray with authority in the name of Jesus.

Here are some helpful suggestions for those who are on a prayer team, especially the family members whose loved one is being prayed for.

1. Meet for prayer first to seek God's wisdom before undertaking an intervention.

When the person is still in denial, unapproachable, or not admitting to a problem and avoiding those seeking to help, then the prayer team should meet to seek divine guidance. If the addict asks for help, seek his permission to schedule a specific time in which the prayer team will help him take the FIRST STEP in petitioning God for an answer to his need.

A number of prayer times may be necessary. If the addict is responsive and is touched by God's Spirit, he may make the decision to accept Christ (if he has not already done so). There will then begin to be visible signs of the person changing. He will need to pray on a daily basis as he begins to take new steps as a follower of Christ. It is important to not give the impression to someone who has taken the FIRST STEP that prayer is a once-done action, and he will now live happily ever after.

In cases where there is no willingness on the part of the addict to receive help of any kind, then the prayer team needs to intercede in prayer fervently and as often as possible in a group, as well as individually in private times of daily devotions.

Pray that the Holy Spirit will bring conviction on this person. Pray for grace and strength for those closest to the person with the problem to be able to deal with how it is affecting them. Pray that some circumstance will take place that will cause the loved one needing help to be either shamed, pained, or awakened to the need for help.

Pray in faith, claiming such biblical promises as the following:

- *"If you need wisdom, ask our generous God, and he will give it to you. He will not rebuke you for asking"* (James 1:5).
- *"For where two or three gather together as my followers, I am there among them"* (Matthew 18:20).
- *"I also pray that you will understand the incredible greatness of God's power for us who believe him. This is the same mighty power that raised Christ from the dead..."* (Ephesians 1:19,20). Remember you are praying for someone spiritually dead. God is still raising the dead today!

If and when the addicted loved one asks for help, ask for God's wisdom in laying out a plan of action. This is when the FIRST STEP by the prayer team can be put into action. No matter whether the addict needs some type of outpatient or residential treatment, ask this person if the prayer team can lay hands on him and pray for him. Through working at a faith-based residential program, I know the difference between those who came for help without spiritual preparation, and those who did. The latter always were able to participate in the chapel services and prayer times better, and in many cases were able to enter immediately into praise and worship.

The first several days in a residential program are critical to the person's response to the program. A person going into a faith-based program who has had spiritual preparation by caring loved ones is more likely to weather the strong temptations to leave during the first days or weeks.

For those who are not in a program, but are willing to go to church: If an addict is invited to be prayed over, be sensitive if the person feels intimidated by the atmosphere. If the individual refuses to be prayed for, it may be good to back off and wait for a second or even third visit to church. Be led by the Holy Spirit. Someone who is being rebellious may need to be pressed and persuaded to seek God's help.

2. Prayers of faith look not for the seen, but the unseen possibilities.

My family prayed for years for an alcoholic loved one. Oh, how those prayers were tested! At times, it seemed the more we prayed, the worse this person became. For most of the years of this person's alcoholism, he held down a good job. But eventually he lost it and ended up nearly a "skid row" type of alcoholic. At his very worst, he cried out to God at a church service. This was totally unexpected by our family; that is, we (especially my mother) believed in his recovery and reclamation, yet when it happened, we were both overjoyed and pleasantly surprised.

It amazes me that when we pray for something to happen, the faith part of us keeps us praying, but the doubt part of us is surprised when the answer finally does come!

This former alcoholic I am referring to was fortunate to have a mother who was always able to look beyond the visible evidence that her son was getting worse to believe in his salvation. In fact, she saw the worsening signs as evidence that he was closer to getting free, and it was actually encouragement to her, rather than discouragement.

> Some mercies are not given to us except in answer to importunate [persistent] prayer. There are blessings that, like ripe fruit, drop into your hand the moment you touch the bough [branch]. But there are others which require you to shake and shake the tree again and again, until you make it rock with the vehemence of your exercise, for only then will the fruit fall.
>
> (CHARLES SPURGEON)

3. **Prayer will enable the loved ones of the addict to stay strong and keep hope alive when there are no visible signs that their loved one wants to change.**

In other words, prayer feeds the soul and keeps faith alive, especially when a loved one's addiction stretches into years, even decades, without an answer. My oldest sister, raised in a Pentecostal preacher's home like myself, left the faith of our family and church and was far from God. She was not an addict, but a working professional. But she bought into all the New Age philosophies. In addition, she was very bitter toward the church and God for certain hurts she experienced in church during her teen years. Mostly she took this bitterness out on my mother.

But Mother never gave up! Years of praying for my sister turned into decades. When she was in her mid sixties and looking forward to retirement and being a world traveler, she succumbed to cancer that took her very quickly. However, I was able to be at her bedside the day she died. When I arrived at the hospital, my sister's Jewish daughter-in-law was reading to her from the Psalms from a Bible. I was able to lead her in a deathbed prayer of repentance and commitment to Christ just hours before her death. On the night she died, I actually slept in my sister's house and saw a Bible on the nightstand next to her bed. I knew she had been reading it, because I noted a mark in the book of Ecclesiastes 3:14: *"And I know that whatever God does is final. Nothing can be added to it or taken from it. God's purpose is that people should fear him."* My sister feared the Lord and accepted Him after fifty years of prayer for her.

I know dozens upon dozens, if not hundreds, of similar stories of the power of persistent prayer for loved ones that was answered in due season. *"So let's not get tired of doing what is good. At just the right time we will reap a harvest of blessing if we don't give up"* (Galatians 6:9).

> I know dozens upon dozens, if not hundreds, of stories of the power of persistent prayer for loved ones that was answered in due season.

The following quote is from Joyce Meyer's book *The Power of Simple Prayer*:

Prayer opens the door for God to work. As we partner with God in the spiritual realm through prayer, we bring things out of that realm into our lives, into our world, into our society, and into the lives of other people. These things that come from heaven, these gifts of God, are already stored up for us, but we will never have them unless we pray and ask God for them. (See 1 Corinthians 2:9.)

4. **Prayer is an act of obedience to God. We ought to pray regardless of the outcome, because God commands it.**

Following a speaking engagement in a certain church, two women approached me, asking for my advice. One woman's son was addicted to heroin and the other woman lost her son to a heroin overdose. I first addressed the mother who lost her son and told her that one of the ways she could deal with her grief was to help the other mother in praying for her son. I said, "You, of all people, can identify with your friend."

I said to the mother whose son was an addict, "You have an excellent prayer partner. Pray together! Stay together!"

These two mothers, however, do serve to remind us that, yes, we pray for answers. We pray because our loved ones need our prayers.

But in the end, we pray regardless of the results, because Christ commands us to pray.

We don't give up on prayer, and we don't give up on God or our faith even in the event of the worst outcome. In fact, we need God and prayer all the more to see us through the valley of the shadow of death.

> In the end, we pray regardless of the results, because Christ commands us to pray. We don't give up on prayer, and we don't give up on God or our faith even in the event of the worst outcome.

In a daily devotional by *Our Daily Bread* entitled "Keep Praying," the following is shared by the writer:

We prayed. Quietly sometimes! Aloud, other times. For more than 17 years we prayed. We prayed for our daughter Melissa's health and direction, for her salvation, and often for her protection. Just as we prayed for our other children, we asked God to have His hand of care on her. As Melissa rolled into her teenage years, we prayed even more that He would keep her from harm—that He would keep His eyes on her as she and her friends began to drive. We prayed, "God, please protect Melissa." So what happened? Didn't God understand how much it would hurt so many people to lose such a beautiful young woman with so much potential for service for Him and others? Didn't God see the other car coming on a warm spring night? We prayed! But Melissa was killed. Now what? Do we stop praying? Do we give up on God? Do we try to make it alone? Absolutely not! Prayer is even more vital now. God—our inexplicable sovereign Lord—is still in control. His commands to pray still stand. His desire to hear from us is still alive. Faith is not demanding what we want; it is trusting God's goodness in spite of life's tragedies. We grieve. We pray. We keep on praying.

(DAVE BRANON, *OUR DAILY BREAD*, FEBRUARY 2007)

Someone reading this may have gone, or is going, through a similar experience. It may be even more painful when loved ones choose to risk their life abusing alcohol or drugs, or both. I encourage you to get involved helping to save others. Perhaps you can ask a few friends to join you in forming a prayer team. You, of all people, would make an excellent prayer team member.

5. **All prayer should be done in connection with Bible reading, especially the Gospels.**

In addition, feed your faith by reading modern-day accounts of how lives have been changed through the power of prayer.

Someone has said, "Feed your faith and your doubts will starve to death." It has been my practice when speaking at a church, banquet, or conference to ask how many have a loved one with a life-controlling problem. It is not unusual for as many as three-quarters of the audience to raise their hands. I then invite them to come forward so I can pray for those loved ones.

The reason I do this is that I always share stories and testimonies of individuals who've had a supernatural encounter with God and were freed from their addiction. These stories encourage and feed the faith of the listeners. In that atmosphere, I invite those who raised their hand on behalf of a son or daughter, spouse, grandchild, sibling, or other relative to be prayed for. It becomes a time when faith is awakened. It is a time when family members are encouraged to not give up on their prodigals—and especially to not give up on prayer.

Praying for loved ones requires persistence, perseverance, and power from God. Our prayers need to be coupled with large faith that God is bigger than anyone's problem, and that we address a loving Father who hears and answers us.

"Keep on asking, and you will receive what you ask for. Keep on seeking, and you will find. Keep on knocking, and the door will be opened to you. For everyone who asks, receives. Everyone who seeks, finds. And to everyone who knocks, the door will be opened. You parents—if your children ask for a loaf of bread, do you give them a stone instead? Or if they ask for a fish, do you give them a snake? Of course not! So if you sinful people know how to give good gifts to your children, how much more will your heavenly Father give good gifts to those who ask him."

(MATTHEW 7:7–11)

Amen!

THE MISSION OF TEEN CHALLENGE

Teen Challenge (TC) is a Christian-based organization. The purpose of TC is to help people who have life-controlling problems and initiate the discipleship process to the point where the student can function as a Christian in society. The TC approach is to teach a whole new way of living by addressing family relationships, work attitudes, self-image and esteem, peer pressure, addictions, social issues, community relationship, and a variety of other life skills. Teen Challenge endeavors to help people become mentally sound, emotionally balanced, socially adjusted, physically well, and spiritually alive.

Teen Challenge is the oldest, largest, and most successful program of its kind in the world.

BROOKLYN TEEN CHALLENGE

Based in Brooklyn, Teen Challenge works with adults whose lives have been impacted by drug addiction and other serious life-controlling problems. The core services of the ministry are the 12–18-month holistic residential recovery program for men and women. Don Wilkerson, the original Co-Founder, is the Director of Brooklyn Teen Challenge.

www.brooklyntc.org

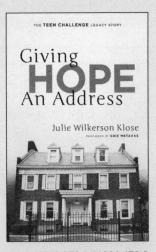